MERRY CHRISTMAS
QUILTS

Oxmoor House®

MERRY CHRISTMAS QUILTS

©1995 by Oxmoor House, Inc.

Book Division of Southern Progress Corporation
P.O. Box 2463, Birmingham, AL 35201

Published by Oxmoor House, Inc., and Leisure Arts, Inc.

All rights reserved. No part of this book may be reproduced in any form or by any means without the prior written permission of the publisher, excepting brief quotations in connection with reviews written specifically for inclusion in magazines or newspapers.

Library of Congress Catalog Number: 95-69204
ISBN: 0-8487-1269-2

Manufactured in the United States of America
Second Printing 1996

Editor-in-Chief: Nancy J. Fitzpatrick
Editorial Director, Special Interest Publications: Ann H. Harvey
Senior Crafts Editor: Susan Ramey Cleveland
Senior Editor, Editorial Services: Olivia Kindig Wells
Art Director: James Boone

MERRY CHRISTMAS QUILTS

Editor: Patricia Wilens
Editorial Assistant: Laura A. Fredericks
Copy Editor: Jennifer K. Mathews
Senior Designer: Larry Hunter
Designer: Carol Loria
Illustrator: Kelly Davis
Publishing Systems Administrator: Rick Tucker
Senior Photographer: John O'Hagan
Photo Stylist: Katie Stoddard
Production and Distribution Director: Phillip Lee
Production Manager: Gail H. Morris
Associate Production Manager: Theresa L. Beste
Production Assistant: Marianne Jordan

Contents

Workshop	4
O Christmas Tree	12
Santa Mini-Quilt	16
Starry Angels	18
Pine Tree Wall Hanging	22
Stepping Stones	26
Christmas Beauty	31
Night Before Christmas	34
Christmas Cactus	36
Visions of Santa	38
Christmas Lily	46

Dear Quilting Friends,

Last year, the 12 members of my bee challenged each other to make a different Santa quilt block each month. At the end of the year we each had enough blocks to make a Santa sampler. Some blocks were pieced, some appliquéd. Some quilters added snowmen, reindeer, stars, trees, and other motifs.

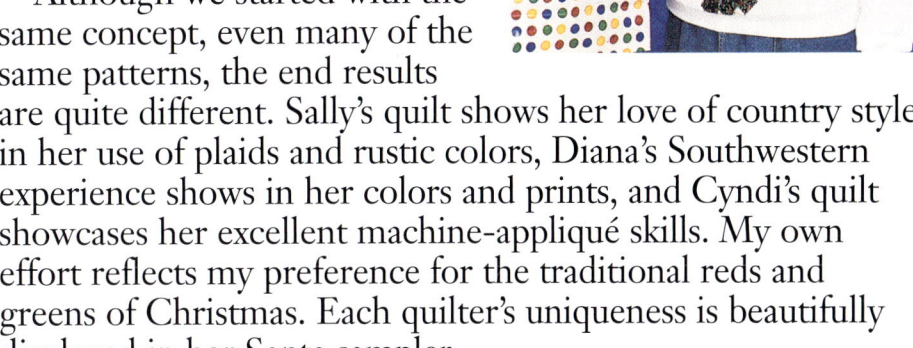

Although we started with the same concept, even many of the same patterns, the end results are quite different. Sally's quilt shows her love of country style in her use of plaids and rustic colors, Diana's Southwestern experience shows in her colors and prints, and Cyndi's quilt showcases her excellent machine-appliqué skills. My own effort reflects my preference for the traditional reds and greens of Christmas. Each quilter's uniqueness is beautifully displayed in her Santa sampler.

One of the patterns in my Santa quilt is presented here—Carol Butzke's *Visions of Santa*, pictured on the cover with instructions beginning on page 38. Another Santa design, Joan Vibert's *Santa Mini-Quilt* on page 16, is both appliquéd and stenciled.

If you prefer angels to Santas, check out Cyndi Wheeler's *Starry Angels* on page 18. Those of you who like more traditional designs might fancy Joanne Cage's *Pine Tree* on page 22 or Annie Phillips's *Stepping Stones* on page 26.

You'll also find Christmas trees, stars, flowers, and more. Just heat up the wassail, polish up your thimble, and get ready to deck your halls with quilted wonders!

Merry stitching,

Susan Ramey Cleveland

WORKSHOP

Selecting Fabrics

The best fabric for quilts is 100% cotton. Yardage requirements are based on 44"-wide fabric and allow for shrinkage. All fabrics, including backing, should be machine-washed, dried, and pressed before cutting. Use warm water and detergent but not fabric softener.

Necessary Notions

- Scissors
- Rotary cutter and mat
- Acrylic rulers
- Template plastic
- Pencils for marking cutting lines
- Sewing needles
- Sewing thread
- Sewing machine
- Seam ripper
- Pins
- Iron and ironing board
- Quilting needles
- Thimble
- Hand quilting thread
- Machine quilting thread

Making Templates

A template is a duplication of a printed pattern, made from a sturdy material, which is traced onto fabric. Many regular shapes such as squares and triangles can be marked directly on the fabric with a ruler, but you need templates for other shapes. Some quiltmakers use templates for all shapes.

You can trace patterns directly onto template plastic. Or make a template by tracing a pattern onto graph paper and gluing the paper to posterboard or sandpaper. (Sandpaper will not slip on fabric.)

When a large pattern is given in two pieces, make one template for the complete piece.

Cut out the template on the marked line. It is important that a template be traced, marked, and cut accurately. If desired, punch out corner dots with a ⅛"-diameter hole punch **(Diagram 1)**.

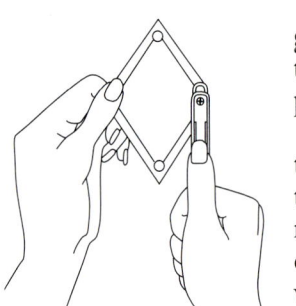

Diagram 1

Mark each template with its letter and grain line. Verify the template's accuracy, placing it over the printed pattern. Any discrepancy, however small, is multiplied many times as the quilt is assembled. Another way to check templates' accuracy is to make a test block before cutting more pieces.

Tracing Templates on Fabric

For hand piecing, templates should be cut to the finished size of the piece so seam lines can be marked on the fabric. Avoiding the selvage, place the template *facedown* on the *wrong* side of the fabric, aligning the template grain line with the straight grain. Hold the template firmly and trace around it. Repeat as needed, leaving ½" between tracings **(Diagram 2)**.

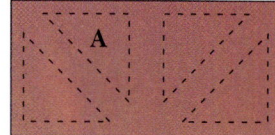

Diagram 2

For machine piecing, templates should include seam allowances. These templates are used in the same manner as for hand piecing, but you can mark the fabric using common lines for efficient cutting **(Diagram 3)**. Mark corners on fabric through holes in the template.

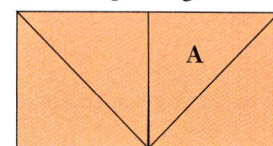

Diagram 3

For hand or machine piecing, use window templates to enhance accuracy by drawing and cutting out both cutting and sewing lines. The guidance of a drawn seam line is very useful for sewing set-in seams, when pivoting at a precise point is critical. Used on the right side of the fabric, window templates help you cut specific motifs with accuracy **(Diagram 4)**.

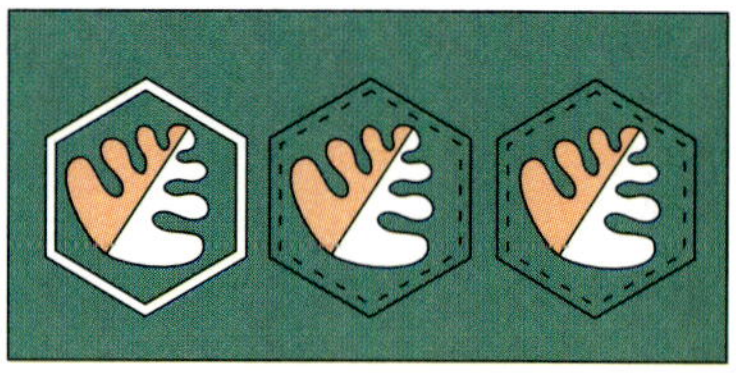

Diagram 4

For hand appliqué, templates should be made the finished size. Place templates *faceup* on the *right* side of the fabric. Position tracings at least ½" apart **(Diagram 5)**. Add a ¼" seam allowance around pieces when cutting.

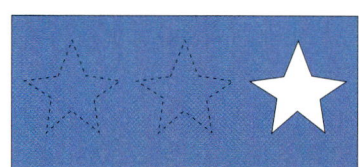

Diagram 5

4

Cutting

Grain Lines

Woven threads form the fabric's grain. Lengthwise grain, parallel to the selvages, has the least stretch; crosswise grain has a little more give.

Long strips such as borders should be cut lengthwise whenever possible and cut first to ensure that you have the necessary length. Usually, other pieces can be cut aligned with either grain.

Bias is the 45° diagonal line between the two grain directions. Bias has the most stretch and is used for curving strips such as flower stems. Bias is often preferred for binding.

Never use the selvage (finished edge). Selvage does not react to washing, drying, and pressing like the rest of the fabric and may pucker when the finished quilt is laundered.

Rotary Cutting

A rotary cutter, used with a protective mat and a ruler, takes getting used to but is very efficient for cutting strips, squares, and triangles. A rotary cutter is fast because you can measure and cut multiple layers with a single stroke, without templates or marking. It is also more accurate than cutting with scissors because fabrics remain flat and do not move during cutting.

Because the blade is very sharp, be sure to get a rotary cutter with a safety guard. Keep the guard in the safe position at all times, except when making a cut. *Always keep the cutter out of the reach of children.*

Use the cutter with a self-healing mat. A good mat for cutting strips is at least 23" wide.

1. Squaring the fabric is the first step in accurate cutting. Fold the fabric with selvages aligned. With the yardage to your right, align a small square ruler with the fold near the cut edge. Place a long ruler against the left side of the square **(Diagram 6).** Keeping the long ruler in place, remove the square. Hold the ruler in place with your left hand as you cut, rolling the cutter *away from you* along the ruler's edge with a steady motion. You can move your left hand along the ruler as you cut, but do not change the position of the ruler. *Keep your fingers away from the ruler's edge when cutting.*

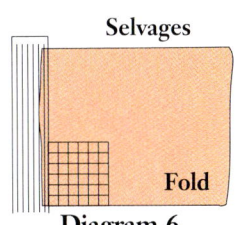

Diagram 6

2. Open the fabric. If the cut was not accurately perpendicular to the fold, the edge will be V-shaped instead of straight **(Diagram 7).** Correct the cut if necessary.

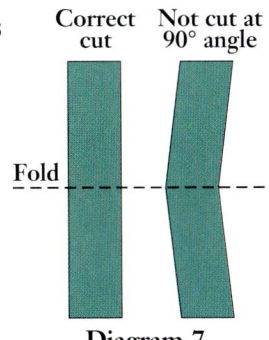

Diagram 7

3. With a transparent ruler, you can measure and cut at the same time. Fold the fabric in half again, aligning the selvages with the fold, making four layers that line up perfectly along the cut edge. Project instructions designate the strip width needed. Position the ruler to measure the correct distance from the edge **(Diagram 8)** and cut. The blade will easily cut through all four layers. Check the strip to be sure the cut is straight. The strip length is the width of the fabric, approximately 43" to 44". Using the ruler again, trim selvages, cutting about ⅜" from each end.

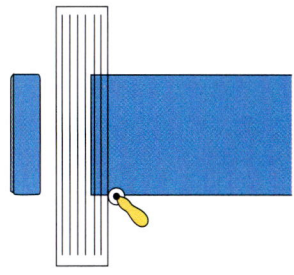

Diagram 8

4. To cut squares and rectangles from a strip, align the desired measurement on the ruler with the strip end and cut across the strip **(Diagram 9).**

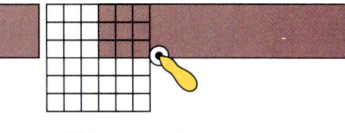

Diagram 9

5. Cut triangles from squares or rectangles. Cutting instructions often direct you to cut a square in half or in quarters diagonally to make right triangles, and this technique can apply to rectangles, too **(Diagram 10).** The outside edges of the square or rectangle are on the straight of the grain, so triangle sides cut on the diagonal are bias.

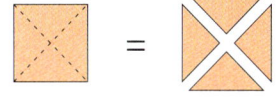

Diagram 10

6. Some projects in this book use a time-saving technique called strip piecing. With this method, strips are joined to make a pieced band. Cut across the seams of this band to cut preassembled units **(Diagram 11).**

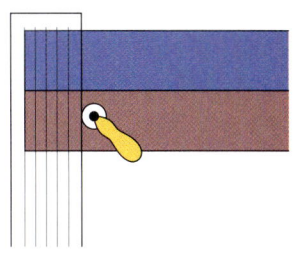

Diagram 11

Machine Piecing

Your sewing machine does not have to be a new, computerized model. A good straight stitch is all that's necessary, but it may be helpful to have a nice satin stitch for appliqué. Clean and oil your machine regularly, use good-quality thread, and replace needles frequently.

1. Patches for machine piecing are cut with the seam allowance included, but the sewing line is not

usually marked. Therefore, a way to make a consistent ¼" seam is essential. Some presser feet have a right toe that is ¼" from the needle. Other machines have an adjustable needle that can be set for a ¼" seam. If your machine has neither feature, experiment to find how the fabric must be placed to make a ¼" seam. Mark this position on the presser foot or throat plate.

2. Use a stitch length that makes a strong seam but is not too difficult to remove with a seam ripper. The best setting is usually 10 to 12 stitches per inch.

3. Pin only when really necessary. If a straight seam is less than 4" and does not have to match an adjoining seam, pinning is not necessary.

4. When intersecting seams must align **(Diagram 12)**, match the units with right sides facing and push a pin through both seams at the seam line. Turn the pinned unit to the right side to check the alignment; then pin securely. As you sew, remove each pin just before the needle reaches it.

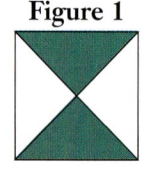
Figure 1
Intersecting seams aligned

Figure 2
Intersecting seams not aligned

Diagram 12

5. Block assembly diagrams are used throughout this book to show how pieces should be joined. Make small units first; then join them in rows and continue joining rows to finish the block **(Diagram 13)**. Blocks are joined in the same manner to complete the quilt top.

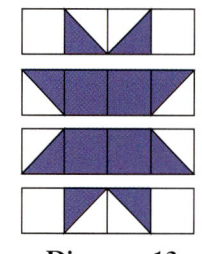
Diagram 13

6. Chain piecing saves time. Stack pieces to be sewn in pairs, with right sides facing. Join the first pair as usual. At the end of the seam, do not backstitch, cut the thread, or lift the presser foot. Just feed in the next pair of pieces—the machine will make a few stitches between pieces before the needle strikes the second piece of fabric. Continue sewing in this way until all pairs are joined. Stack the chain of pieces until you are ready to clip them apart **(Diagram 14)**.

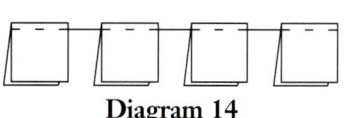
Diagram 14

7. Most seams are sewn straight across, from raw edge to raw edge. Since they will be crossed by other seams, they do not require backstitching to secure them.

8. When piecing diamonds or other angled seams, you may need to make set-in seams. For these, always mark the corner dots (shown on the patterns) on the fabric pieces. Stitch one side, starting at the outside edge and being careful not to sew beyond the dot into the seam allowance **(Diagram 15, Figure A)**. Backstitch. Align the other side of the piece as needed, with right sides facing. Sew from the dot to the outside edge **(Figure B)**.

9. Sewing curved seams requires extra care. First, mark the centers of both the convex (outward) and concave (inward) curves **(Diagram 16)**. Staystitch just inside the seam allowance of both pieces. Clip the concave piece to the stitching **(Figure A)**. With right sides facing and raw edges aligned, pin the two patches together at the center **(Figure B)** and at the left edge **(Figure C)**. Sew from edge to center, stopping frequently to check that the raw edges are aligned. Stop at the center with the needle down. Raise the presser foot and pin the pieces together from the center to the right edge. Lower the foot and continue to sew. Press seam allowances toward the concave curve **(Figure D)**.

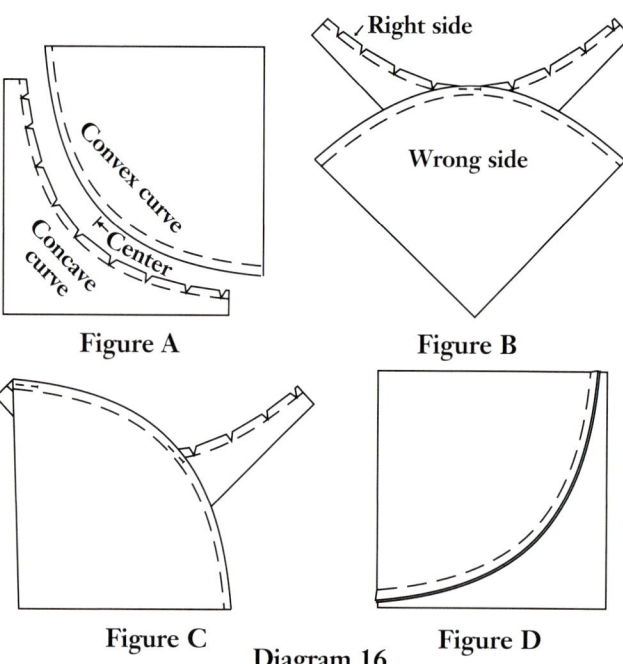
Figure A
Figure B
Figure C
Figure D
Diagram 16

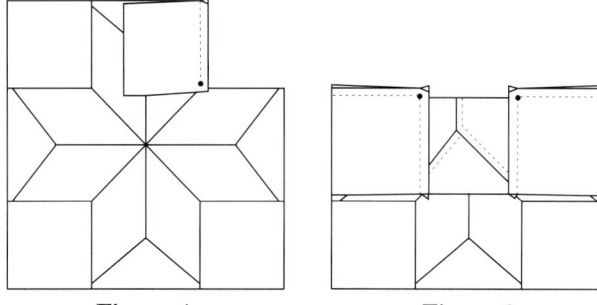
Figure 1
Figure 2
Diagram 15

Hand Piecing

Make a running stitch of 8 to 10 stitches per inch along the marked seam line on the wrong side of the fabric. Don't pull the fabric as you sew; let the pieces lie relaxed in your hand. Sew from seam line to seam line, not from edge to edge as in machine piecing.

When ending a line of stitching, backstitch over the last stitch and make a loop knot **(Diagram 17)**.

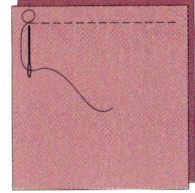
Diagram 17

Match seams and points accurately, pinning patches together before piecing. Align match points as described in Step 4 under Machine Piecing.

When joining units where several seams meet, do not sew over seam allowances; sew *through* them at the match point **(Diagram 18)**. When four or more seams meet, press the seam allowances in the same direction to reduce bulk **(Diagram 19)**.

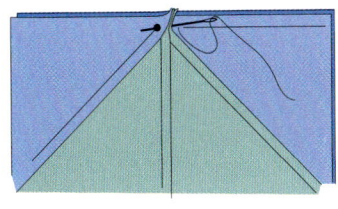
Diagram 18

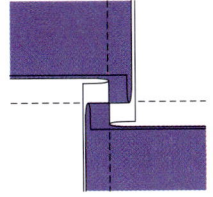
Diagram 19

Pressing

Careful pressing is necessary for precise piecing. Press each seam as you go. Sliding the iron back and forth may push the seam out of shape. Use an up-and-down motion, lifting the iron from spot to spot. Press the seam flat on the wrong side. Open the piece and, on the right side, press both seam allowances to one side (usually toward the darker fabric). Pressing the seam open leaves tiny gaps through which batting may beard.

Appliqué

Traditional Hand Appliqué

Hand appliqué requires that you turn under a seam allowance around the shape to prevent frayed edges.

1. Trace around the template on the right side of the fabric. This line indicates where to turn the seam allowance. Cut each piece approximately ¼" outside the line.

2. For simple shapes, turn the edges by pressing the seam allowance to the back; complex shapes may require basting the seam allowance. Sharp points and strong curves are best appliquéd with freezer paper. Clip curves to make a smooth edge. With practice, you can work without pressing seam allowances, turning edges under with the needle as you sew.

3. Do not turn under any seam allowance that will be covered by another appliqué piece.

4. To stitch, use one strand of cotton-wrapped polyester sewing thread in a color that matches the appliqué. Use a slipstitch, but keep the stitch very small on the surface. Working from right to left (or left to right if you're left-handed), pull the needle through the base fabric and catch only a few threads on the folded edge of the appliqué. Reinsert the needle into the base fabric, under the top thread on the appliqué edge to keep the thread from tangling **(Diagram 20)**.

5. An alternative to slipstitching is to work a decorative buttonhole stitch around each figure **(Diagram 21)**.

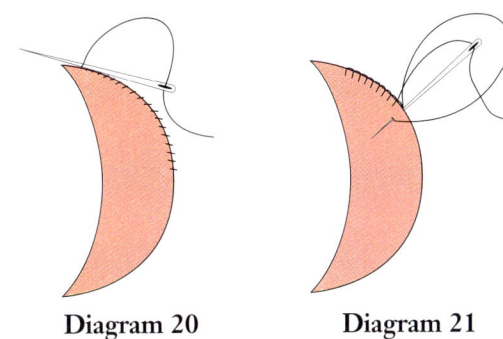
Diagram 20   Diagram 21

Freezer Paper Hand Appliqué

Supermarket freezer paper saves time because it eliminates the need for basting seam allowances.

1. Trace the template onto the *dull* side of the freezer paper and cut the paper on the marked line. *Note:* If a design is not symmetrical, turn the template over and trace a mirror image so the fabric piece won't be reversed when you cut it out.

2. Pin the freezer-paper shape, with its *shiny side* up, to the *wrong side* of the fabric. Following the paper shape and adding a scant ¼" seam allowance, cut out the fabric piece. Do not remove pins.

3. Using just the tip of a dry iron, press the seam allowance to the shiny side of the paper. Be careful not to touch the freezer paper with the iron.

4. Appliqué the piece to the background as in traditional appliqué. Trim the fabric from behind the shape, leaving ¼" seam allowances. Separate the freezer paper from the fabric with your fingernail and pull gently to remove it. If you prefer not to trim the background fabric, pull out the freezer paper before you complete stitching.

5. Sharp points require special attention. Turn the point down and press it **(Diagram 22, Figure A)**. Fold the seam allowance on one side over the point and press **(Figure B)**; then fold the other seam allowance over the point and press **(Figure C)**.

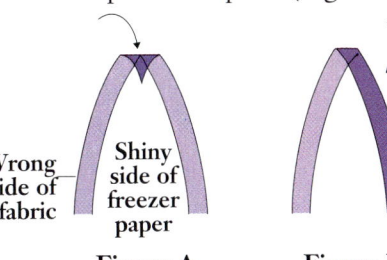

Figure A   Figure B   Figure C

Diagram 22

6. When pressing curved edges, clip sharp inward curves **(Diagram 23)**. If the shape doesn't curve smoothly, separate the paper from the fabric with your fingernail and try again.

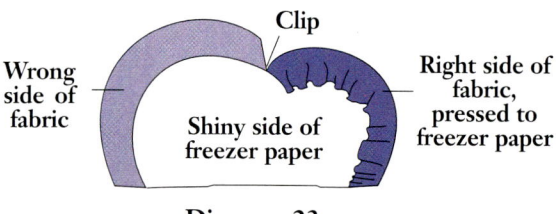

Diagram 23

7. Remove the pins when all seam allowances have been pressed to the freezer paper. Position the prepared appliqué right side up on the background fabric. Press to adhere it to the background fabric.

Machine Appliqué

A machine-sewn satin stitch makes a neat edging. For machine appliqué, cut appliqué pieces without adding seam allowances.

Using fusible web to adhere pieces to the background adds a stiff extra layer to the appliqué and is not appropriate for some quilts. It is best used on small pieces, difficult fabrics, or for wall hangings and accessories in which added stiffness is acceptable. The web prevents fraying and shifting during appliqué.

Place tear-away stabilizer under the background fabric behind the appliqué. Machine-stitch the appliqué edges with a satin stitch or close-spaced zigzag **(Diagram 24)**. Test the stitch length and width on a sample first. Use an open-toed presser foot. Remove the stabilizer when appliqué is complete.

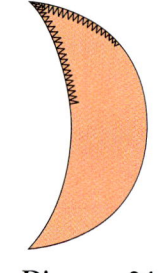

Diagram 24

Measuring Borders

Because seams may vary and fabrics may stretch a bit, opposite sides of your assembled quilt top may not be the same measurement. You can (and should) correct this when you add borders.

Measure the length of each side of the quilt. Trim the side border strips to match the *shorter* of the two sides. Join borders to the quilt as described below, easing the longer side of the quilt to fit the border. Join borders to the top and bottom edges in the same manner.

Straight Borders

Side borders are usually added first **(Diagram 25)**. With right sides facing and raw edges aligned, pin the center of one border strip to the center of one side of

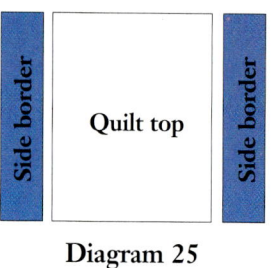

Diagram 25

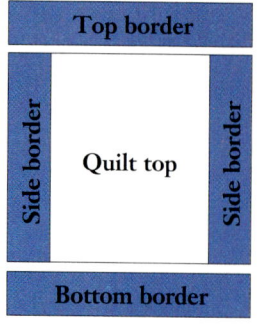

Diagram 26

the quilt top. Pin the border to the quilt at each end and then pin along the side as desired. Machine-stitch with the border strip on top. Press the seam allowance toward the border. Trim excess border fabric at each end. In the same manner, add the border to the opposite side and then the top and bottom borders **(Diagram 26)**.

Mitered Borders

1. Measure your quilt sides. Trim the side border strips to fit the shorter side *plus* the width of the border *plus* 2".
2. Center the measurement of the shorter side on one border strip, placing a pin at each end and at the center of the measurement.
3. With right sides facing and raw edges aligned, match the pins on the border strip to the center and corners of the longer side of the quilt. (Border fabric will extend beyond the corners.)
4. Start machine-stitching at the top pin, backstitching to lock the stitches. Continue to sew, easing the quilt between pins. Stop at the last pin and backstitch. Join remaining borders in the same manner. Press seam allowances toward borders.
5. With right sides facing, fold the quilt diagonally, aligning the raw edges of adjacent borders. Pin securely **(Diagram 27)**.

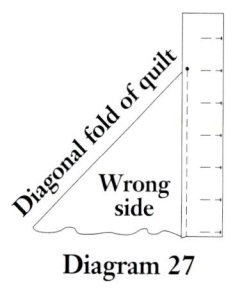

Diagram 27

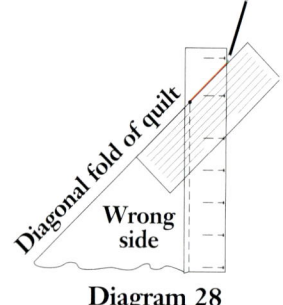

Diagram 28

6. Align a yardstick or quilter's ruler along the diagonal fold **(Diagram 28)**. Holding the ruler firmly, mark a line from the end of the border seam to the raw edge.
7. Start machine-stitching at the beginning of the marked line, backstitch, and then stitch on the line out to the raw edge.

8. Unfold the quilt to be sure that the corner lies flat. Correct the stitching if necessary. Trim the seam allowance to ¼".

9. Miter the remaining corners in the same manner. Press the corner seams open.

Quilting Without Marking

Some quilts can be quilted in-the-ditch (right along the seam line), outline-quilted (¼" from the seam line), or echo-quilted (lines of quilting rippling outward from the design like waves on a pond). These methods can be used without any marking at all. If you are machine quilting, simply use the edge of your presser foot and the seam line as a guide. If you are hand quilting, by the time you have pieced a quilt top, your eye will be practiced enough for you to produce straight, even quilting without the guidance of marked lines.

Marking Quilting Designs

Many quilters like to mark the entire top at one time, a practice that requires long-lasting markings. The most common tool for this purpose is a sharp **pencil**. However, most pencils are made with an oil-based graphite lead, which often will not wash out completely. Look for a high-quality artist's pencil marked "2H" or higher (the higher the number, the harder the lead, and the lighter the line it will make). Sharpen the pencil frequently to keep the line on the fabric thin and light. Or try a mechanical pencil with a 0.5-mm lead. It will maintain a fine line without sharpening.

While you are in the art supply store, get a **white plastic eraser** (brand name Magic Rub). This eraser, used by professional drafters and artists, will cleanly remove the carbon smudges left by pencil lead without fraying the fabric or leaving eraser crumbs.

Water- and **air-soluble marking pens** are convenient, but controversial, marking tools. Some quilters have found that the marks reappear, often up to several years later, while others have no problems with them.

Be sure to test these pens on each fabric you plan to mark and *follow package directions exactly*. Because the inks can be permanently set by heat, be very careful with a marked quilt. Do not leave it in your car on a hot day and never touch it with an iron until the marks have been removed. Plan to complete the quilting within a year after marking it with a water-soluble pen.

Air-soluble pens are best for marking small sections at a time. The marks disappear within 24 to 48 hours, but the ink remains in the fabric until it is washed. After the quilt is completed and before it is used, rinse it twice in clear, cool water, using no soap, detergent, or bleach. Let the quilt air-dry.

For dark fabrics, the cleanest marker you can use is a thin sliver of pure, white **soap**. Choose a soap that contains no creams, deodorants, dyes, or perfumes; these added ingredients may leave a residue on the fabric.

Other marking tools include **colored pencils** made specifically for marking fabric and **tailor's chalk** (available in powdered, stick, and traditional cake form). When using chalk, mark small sections of the quilt at a time because the chalk rubs off easily.

Quilting Stencils

Quilting patterns can be purchased as precut stencils. Simply lay these on your quilt top and mark the design through the cutout areas.

To make your own stencil of a printed quilting pattern, such as the one below, use a permanent marker to trace the design onto a blank sheet of template plastic. Then use a craft knife to cut out the design.

Quilting Stencil Pattern

Making a Quilt Backing

Some fabric and quilt shops sell 90" and 108" widths of 100% cotton fabric that are very practical for quilt backing. However, the instructions in this book always give backing yardage based on 44"-wide fabric.

When using 44"-wide fabric, all quilts wider than 41" will require a pieced backing. For quilts 41" to 80" wide, you will need an amount of fabric equal to two times the desired *length* of the unfinished backing. (The unfinished backing should be at least 3" larger on all sides than the quilt top.)

The simplest method of making a backing is to cut the fabric in half widthwise **(Diagram 29),** and then sew the two panels together lengthwise. This results in a backing with a vertical center seam. Press the seam allowances to one side.

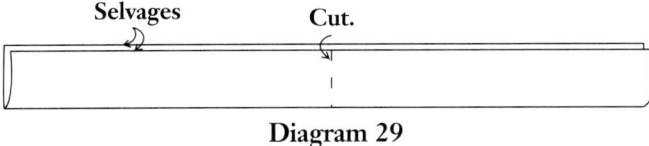

Diagram 29

Another method of seaming the backing results in two vertical seams and a center panel of fabric. This method is often preferred by quilt show judges. Begin by cutting the fabric in half widthwise. Open the two lengths and stack them, with right sides facing and selvages aligned. Stitch along *both* selvage edges to create a tube of fabric **(Diagram 30).** Cut down the center of the top layer of fabric only and open the fabric flat **(Diagram 31).** Press seam allowances to one side.

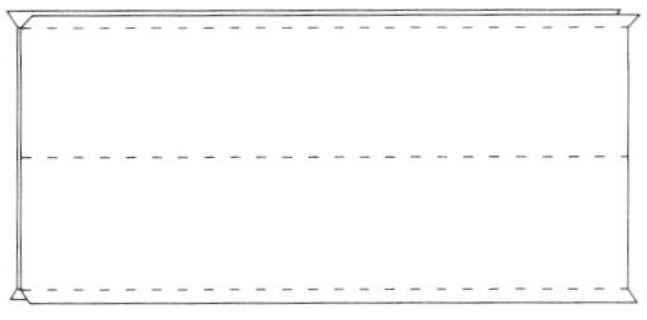

If the quilt is wider than 80", it is more economical to cut the fabric into three lengths that are the desired width of the backing. Join the three lengths so that the seams are horizontal to the quilt, rather than vertical. For this method, you'll need an amount of fabric equal to three times the *width* of the unfinished backing.

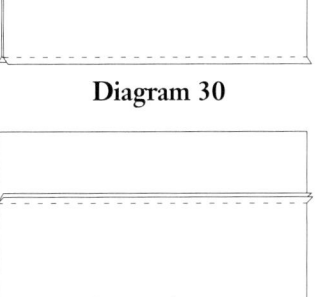

Diagram 30

Diagram 31

Fabric requirements in this book reflect the most economical method of seaming the backing fabric.

Layering and Basting

After the quilt top and backing are made, the next steps are layering and basting in preparation for quilting.

Prepare a large working surface to spread out the quilt—a large table, two tables pushed together, or the floor. Place the backing on the working surface wrong side up. Unfold the batting and place it on top of the backing, smoothing away any wrinkles or lumps.

Lay the quilt top wrong side down on top of the batting and backing. Make sure the edges of the backing and quilt top are parallel.

Knot a long strand of sewing thread and use a long (darning) needle for basting. Begin basting in the center of the quilt and baste out toward the edges. The basting stitches should cover an ample amount of the quilt so that the layers do not shift during quilting.

Machine quilters use nickel-plated safety pins for basting so there will be no basting threads to get caught on the presser foot. Safety pins, spaced approximately 4" apart, can be used by hand quilters, too.

Hand Quilting

Hand-quilted stitches should be evenly spaced, with the spaces between stitches about the same length as the stitches themselves. The *number* of stitches per inch is less important than the *uniformity* of the stitching. Don't worry if you take only five or six stitches per inch; just be consistent throughout the project.

Machine Quilting

For machine quilting, the backing and batting should be 3" larger all around than the quilt top, because the quilting process pushes the quilt top fabric outward. After quilting, trim the backing and batting to the same size as the quilt top.

Thread your bobbin with good-quality sewing thread (not quilting thread) in a color to match the backing. Use a top thread color to match the quilt top or use invisible nylon thread.

An even-feed or walking foot will feed all the quilt's layers through the machine at the same speed. It is possible to machine-quilt without this foot (by experimenting with tension and presser foot pressure), but it will be much easier *with* it. If you do not have this foot, get one from your sewing machine dealer.

Straight-Grain Binding

1. Mark the fabric in horizontal lines the width of the binding **(Diagram 32)**.

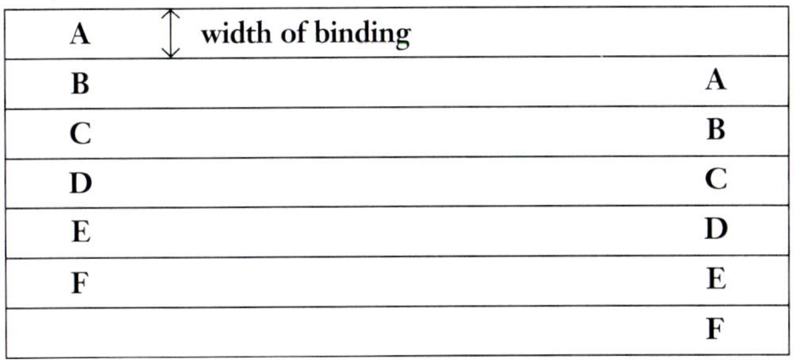

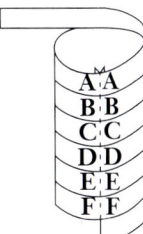

Diagram 32

2. With right sides facing, fold the fabric in half, offsetting drawn lines by matching letters and raw edges **(Diagram 33)**. Stitch a ¼" seam.

3. Cut the binding in a continuous strip, starting with one end and following the marked lines around the tube. Press the strip in half lengthwise.

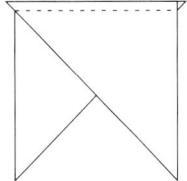

Diagram 33

Continuous Bias Binding

This technique can be used to make continuous bias for appliqué as well as for binding.

1. Cut a square of fabric in half diagonally to form two triangles. With right sides facing, join the triangles **(Diagram 34)**. Press the seam allowance open.

2. Mark parallel lines the desired width of the binding **(Diagram 35)**, taking care not to stretch the bias. With right sides facing, align the raw edges (indicated as Seam 2). As you align the edges, offset one Seam 2 point past its natural matching point by one line. Stitch the seam; then press the seam allowance open.

3. Cut the binding in a continuous strip, starting with the protruding point and following the marked lines around the tube **(Diagram 36)**. Press the strip in half lengthwise.

Diagram 34

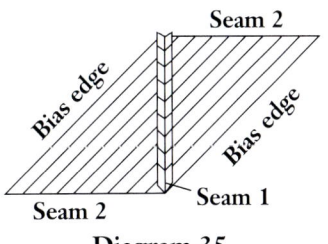

Diagram 35

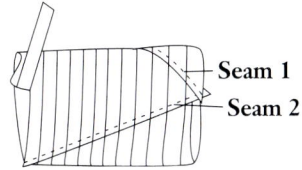

Diagram 36

Applying Binding

Binding is applied to the front of the quilt first. You may begin anywhere on the edge of the quilt except at the corner.

1. Matching raw edges, lay the binding on the quilt. Fold down the top corner of the binding at a 45° angle, align the raw edges, and pin **(Diagram 37)**.

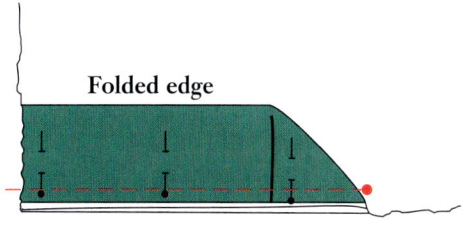

Diagram 37

2. Beginning at the folded end, machine-stitch the binding to the quilt. Stop stitching ¼" from the corner and backstitch. Fold the binding strip diagonally away from the quilt, making a 45° angle **(Diagram 38)**.

3. Fold the binding strip straight down along the next side to be stitched, creating a pleat in the corner. Position the needle at the ¼" seam line of the new side **(Diagram 39)**. Make a few stitches, backstitch, and then stitch the seam. Continue until all corners and sides are done. Overlap the end of the binding strip over the beginning fold and stitch about 2" beyond it. Trim any excess binding.

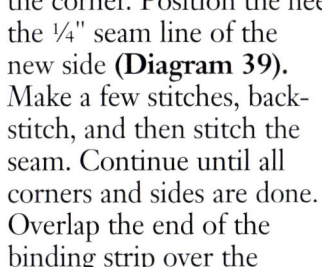

Diagram 38

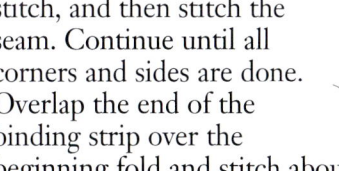

Diagram 39

4. Turn the binding over the raw edge of the quilt. Slipstitch it in place on the back, using thread that matches the binding. The fold at the beginning of the binding strip will create a neat, angled edge when it is folded to the back.

5. At each corner, fold the binding to form a miter **(Diagram 40)**. Hand-stitch the miters closed if desired.

Diagram 40

Quilt by The Vanessa-Ann Collection
Ogden, Utah

O Christmas Tree

The patchwork and sashing in this wall hanging capture the lovely look of a tree framed in a neighbor's window during the holiday season. You'll find yourself humming the beloved Christmas melody as you stitch it.

Finished Quilt Size
27" x 33"

Number of Blocks and Finished Size
12 blocks   5" x 5"

Fabric Requirements
Red print	⅛ yard
Green print	¼ yard
Dark green print	¼ yard
Dark green pindot	1 yard*
Tan pindot	1¼ yards

*Includes fabric for binding.

Number to Cut**
Template A	4 red print
Template A rev.	4 red print
Template B	2 green print
	2 dark green print
Template C	2 green print
Template D	3 green print
	1 dark green print
Template E	6 green print
	14 dark green print
Template F	5 dark green pindot
Template G	1 dark green print
Template H	2 green print
Template I	2 green print
Template J	2 green print
	3 dark green print
Template J rev.	2 green print
	3 dark green print
5½" square (K)	2 green print

**See Step 1 to cut backing, borders, and sashing before cutting other pieces.

Quilt Top Assembly

1. From tan pindot, cut 1 (30" x 36") piece for backing, 2 (2" x 35") and 2 (2" x 29") strips for inner border, 3 (2" x 18½") strips for horizontal sashing, and 8 (2" x 5½") for vertical sashing. From dark green pindot, cut 2 (3" x 35") and 2 (3" x 29") strips for outer border. Set aside.

2. For star block, join each A to 1 A rev. along 1 short edge as shown in **Diagram 1,** making 4 V-shaped units. Be careful not to stitch into seam allowance. Set dark green D into V of 1 A/A unit. (See page 6, Step 8, for tips on sewing set-in seams.) Set green print Ds into remaining A/A units.

3. Referring to **Diagram 2,** join dark green Bs to both sides of unit with dark green D. Join light green Bs to 2 A/A units. Join units in pairs as shown to make 2 halves of star. Stitch diagonal seam to join halves. Set in Cs at top corners.

4. Refer to **Diagram 3** to piece remaining blocks. For Row 2, join light green Js to dark green Es; then join 2 E/J units to make block for left side of row. Using J rev. pieces, repeat to make block for right side. Make side blocks for rows 3 and 4 in same manner, joining light green Es and dark green Js as shown. For Row 4, join E/J units to I rectangles.

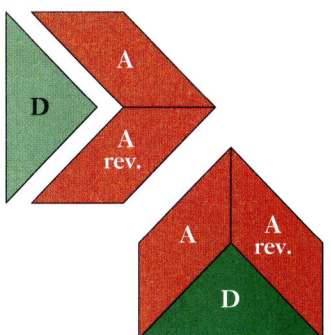

Diagram 1

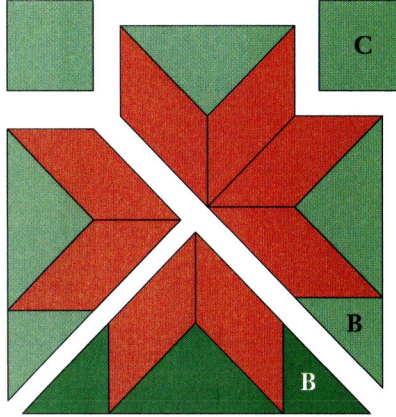

Diagram 2

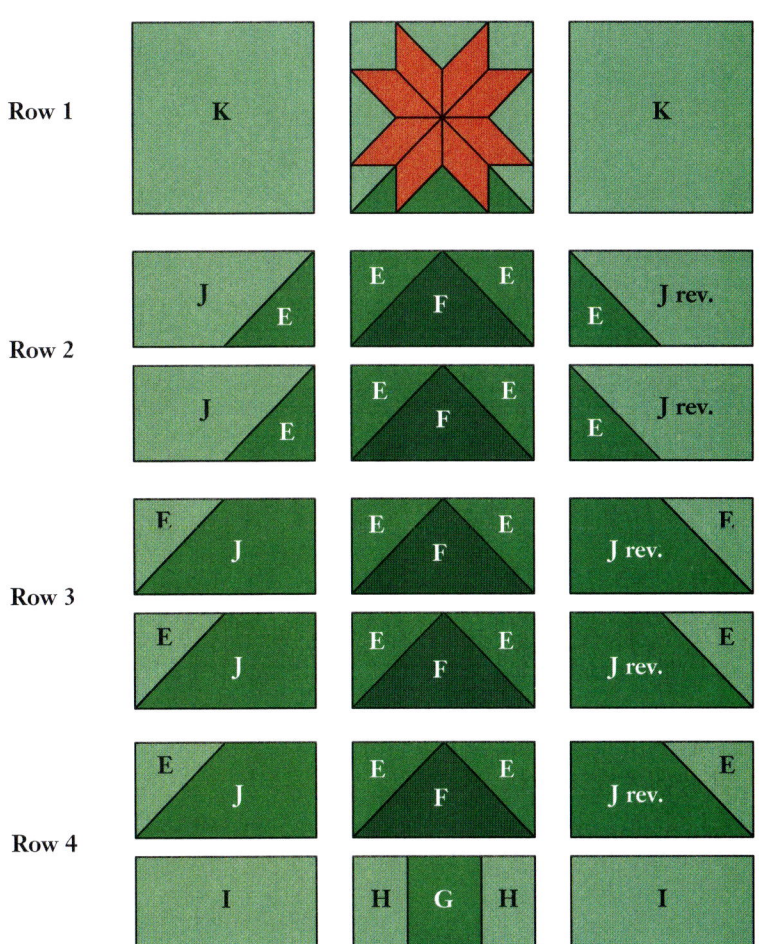

Diagram 3

5. To make center blocks for rows 2, 3, and 4, join dark green Es to Fs. Join 2 E/F units to make 1 block for each of rows 2 and 3. For Row 4, join Hs to sides of G; then join G/H unit to remaining E/F unit to complete block.

6. Arrange blocks in 4 rows as shown in **Diagram 3,** adding a 5½" sashing strip between blocks. Join blocks and strips in each row. Referring to photograph, join rows, sewing 18½" sashing strips between rows.

7. Match each tan border strip with a green pindot strip of same length. Join each pair along 1 long edge to get 2 (35") border units and 2 (29") border units. Join long border units to quilt sides; then join short units to top and bottom edges, mitering corners.

Quilting

The quilt shown has a poinsettia design quilted in each border corner. Make a stencil from poinsettia pattern on this page and mark design on quilt. Layer backing, batting, and quilt top; then baste. Outline-quilt patchwork and marked border design. Add other quilting as desired.

Finishing

Referring to instructions on page 11, make 3½ yards of 2"-wide bias or straight-grain binding from green pindot. Apply binding to quilt edges.

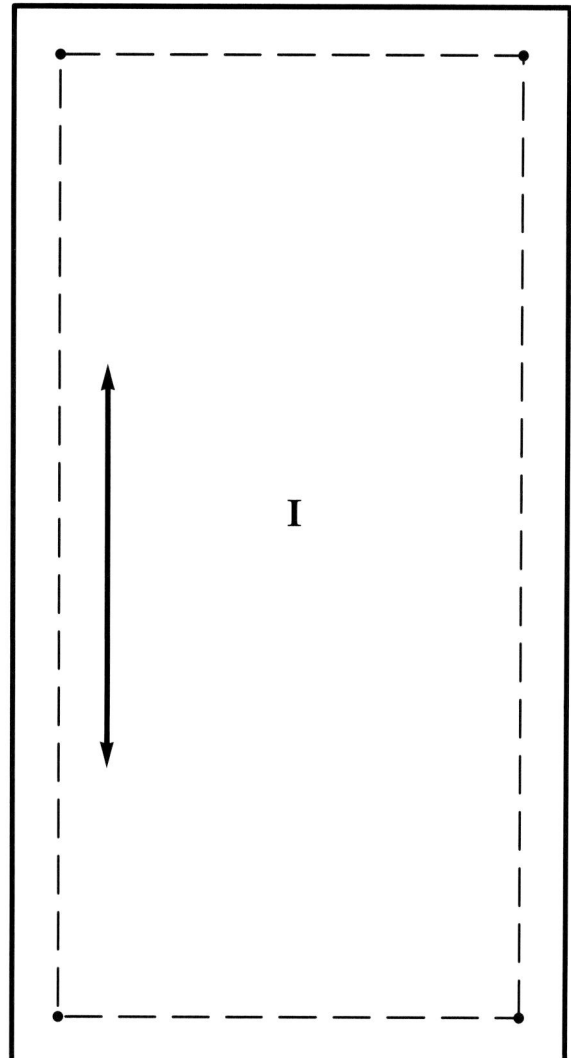

Poinsettia Quilting Pattern

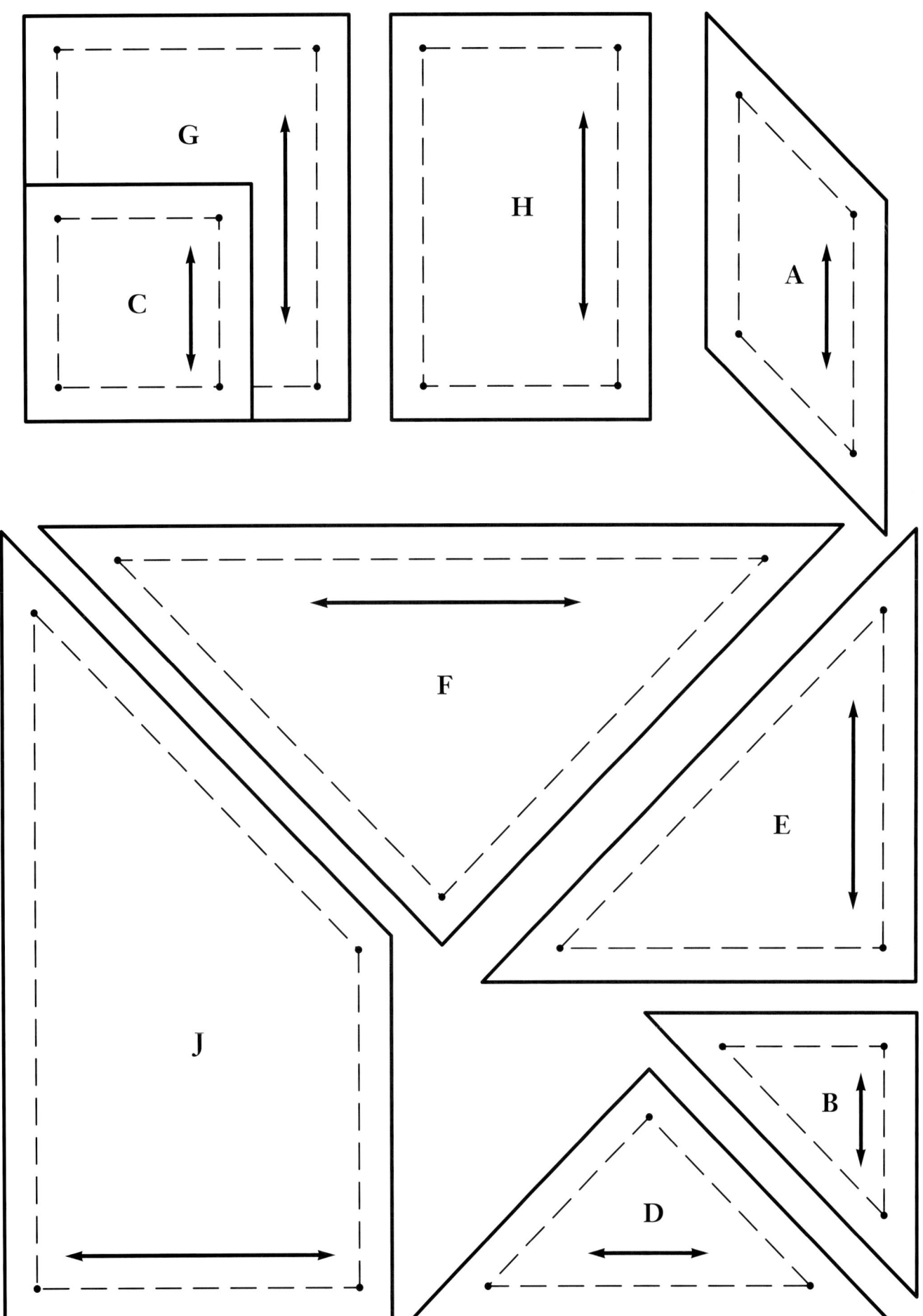

*Quilt by Joan Vibert
Ottawa, Kansas*

Santa Mini-Quilt

Bring folk art charm to the smallest nook or cranny of your holiday home with this miniature wall hanging or table topper. A delightful pairing of appliqué and fabric stenciling, the piece achieves an antiqued look with dark, homespun-type fabrics.

Finished Quilt Size
8½" x 12½"

Number of Blocks and Finished Size
4 blocks   3" x 5"

Fabric Requirements
Red   scraps
Muslin   scraps
Black print   ⅛ yard
Tan   ⅛ yard
Red/black stripe   ⅓ yard*

*Includes fabric for backing.

Other Materials
2 (3" x 5") pieces of stencil plastic
Craft knife
Small stencil brush
Black, red, white fabric paints
Black embroidery floss

Number to Cut**
Template A   1 red
Template A rev.   1 red
Template B   1 muslin
Template B rev.   1 muslin
Template C   1 red
Template C rev.   1 red
Template D   1 black print
Template D rev.   1 black print
Template E   1 black print
Template E rev.   1 black print
3½" x 5½"   4 tan

**See Step 1 to cut borders and backing before cutting other pieces.

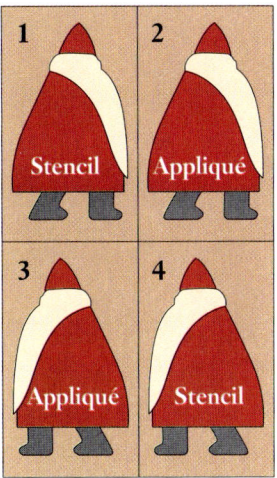

Blocks Diagram

Quilt Top Assembly
1. From stripe, cut 2 (1¼" x 10½") lengthwise strips and 2 (1¼" x 8") lengthwise strips for inner border. Also from stripe, cut 1 (9" x 13") piece for backing. From black print, cut 2 (1" x 12") and 2 (1" x 9½") strips for outer border. Set aside.

2. Prepare pieces for appliqué. (See pages 7 and 8 for tips on hand and machine appliqué.)

3. For Block 2 (as shown in **Blocks Diagram**), use full-size pattern as a guide to position hat (A) and boots (D and E) on 1 tan rectangle. Appliqué; then stitch coat (C) in place. Position and appliqué beard last. Repeat with reversed pieces to make Block 3.

4. For stenciling, lay plastic over full-size pattern and cut 1 stencil for boots and beard; then cut a second stencil for coat and hat.

Practice stenciling on fabric scraps, using small amounts of paint and a nearly dry brush. When satisfied with results, proceed to stencil santa blocks.

5. For Block 1, stencil hat and coat in red on 1 tan rectangle. Clean paint from stencil surface; then reverse stencil and repeat for Block 4. When red paint is completely dry, stencil beards in white and boots in black. Let dry.

6. Heat-set paint by pressing wrong side of fabric with a hot, dry iron.

7. Join blocks 1 and 2; then join blocks 3 and 4. Join blocks as shown.

8. Sew longer striped border strips to quilt sides; then stitch remaining strips to top and bottom edges. Repeat for black outer border.

Finishing
1. With right sides facing, stitch top to backing, leaving a 2" opening at center bottom. Clip corners and turn. Whipstitch opening closed.

2. Cut 18" of embroidery floss. Referring to photograph, make a stitch at quilt center through all layers. Clip thread, leaving 2" tails on top of quilt at both ends of stitch. Knot thread; then clip tails to 1". Repeat at border corners and at block corners as desired, rethreading needle as necessary.

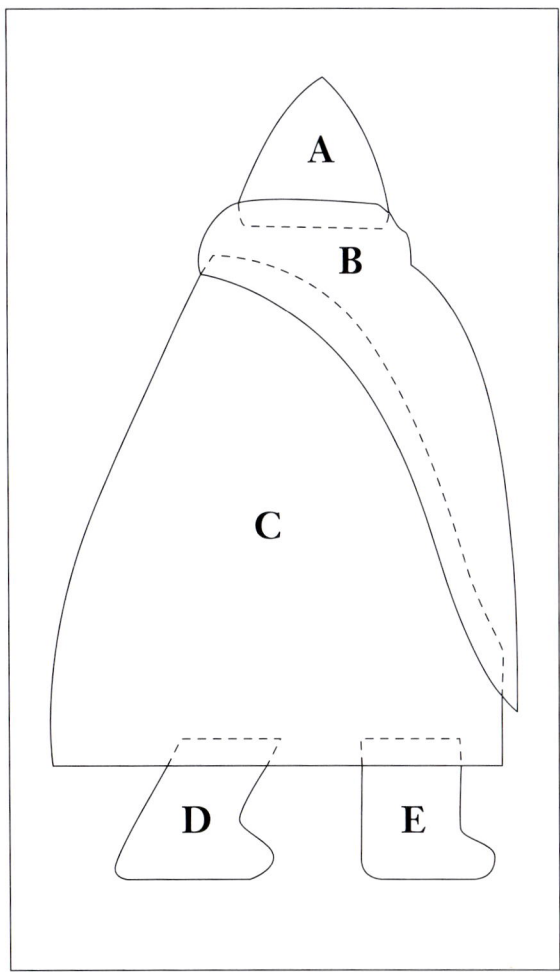

Full-Size Patterns and Placement Diagram

*Quilt and pillows by Cynthia Moody Wheeler
Birmingham, Alabama*

Starry Angels

A choir of appliquéd angels heralds the yuletide season every time you hang this heavenly little quilt. Add a touch of glamour with a glimmer of lamé and sparkling gold thread. Use the same patterns to make pillows or other decorator accessories.

Finished Quilt Size
48" x 48"

Number of Blocks and Finished Size
9 blocks   10" x 10"

Fabric Requirements
Gold-on-white
   pindot   1 yard
Dark green   1 yard*
Green print   1¼ yards
Green stripe   1½ yards
Gold lamé   ⅛ yard
Backing   3 yards

*Includes fabric for binding.

Other Materials
Paper-backed
   fusible web   1 yard
Tear-away
   stabilizer   1 yard
100%-cotton fusible
   interfacing   ⅛ yard
Gold metallic sewing thread
Removable fabric marker

Number to Cut
10½" squares   9 pindot
9½" squares   5 dark green

Setting Diagram

Quilt Top Assembly

Note: The following instructions are for machine appliqué as shown. For hand appliqué, make templates from angel patterns on page 20, add seam allowances when cutting out fabric pieces, and disregard references to fusible web and tear-away stabilizer.

1. Soak cotton interfacing in warm water; then let drip-dry. Following manufacturer's instructions, fuse interfacing to wrong side of lamé.

2. Trace 5 angel halos onto paper side of a 5" x 9" piece of fusible web. Fuse web to wrong side of interfaced lamé. Following drawn lines, cut out 5 halos.

3. In same manner, trace 5 angels (without halos) onto remaining fusible web. Fuse web for 1 angel to wrong side of each dark green square. Cut out angel pieces. Remove paper backings from all cut pieces.

4. Center pieces for 1 angel on each of 5 pindot squares and fuse in place. Cut a square of stabilizer to match each pindot square and pin to wrong side of fabric.

5. Thread sewing machine with metallic thread on top and white thread in bobbin. Adjust stitch width for satin stitch. Appliqué around each piece.

6. Center each of 4 remaining pindot squares over star pattern on page 21. Using fabric marker, lightly trace star and rays.

7. From green print, cut 2 (2¼" x 34") strips and 6 (2¼" x 10½") strips for sashing. Referring to **Setting Diagram,** lay out blocks in 3 vertical rows of 3 blocks with short sashing strips between blocks. Join blocks and sashing in each row. Press seam allowances toward sashing. Join rows and vertical sashing as shown.

8. From remaining green print, cut 2 (2¼" x 34") strips and 2 (2¼" x 38") strips for inner border. Join shorter strips to top and bottom edges of quilt. Press seam allowances toward border. Join long strips to quilt sides.

9. From dark green, cut 4 (1½" x 40") strips for middle border. Join to quilt in same manner as for inner border.

10. From stripe, cut 4 (5" x 50") lengthwise strips for outer border. Join borders to quilt, mitering corners.

Quilting
Use metallic thread to quilt marked stars. Outline-quilt blocks and sashing; then quilt borders as desired.

Finishing
Referring to instructions on page 11, make 5¾ yards of 2½"-wide bias or straight-grain binding from remaining dark green. Apply binding to quilt edges.

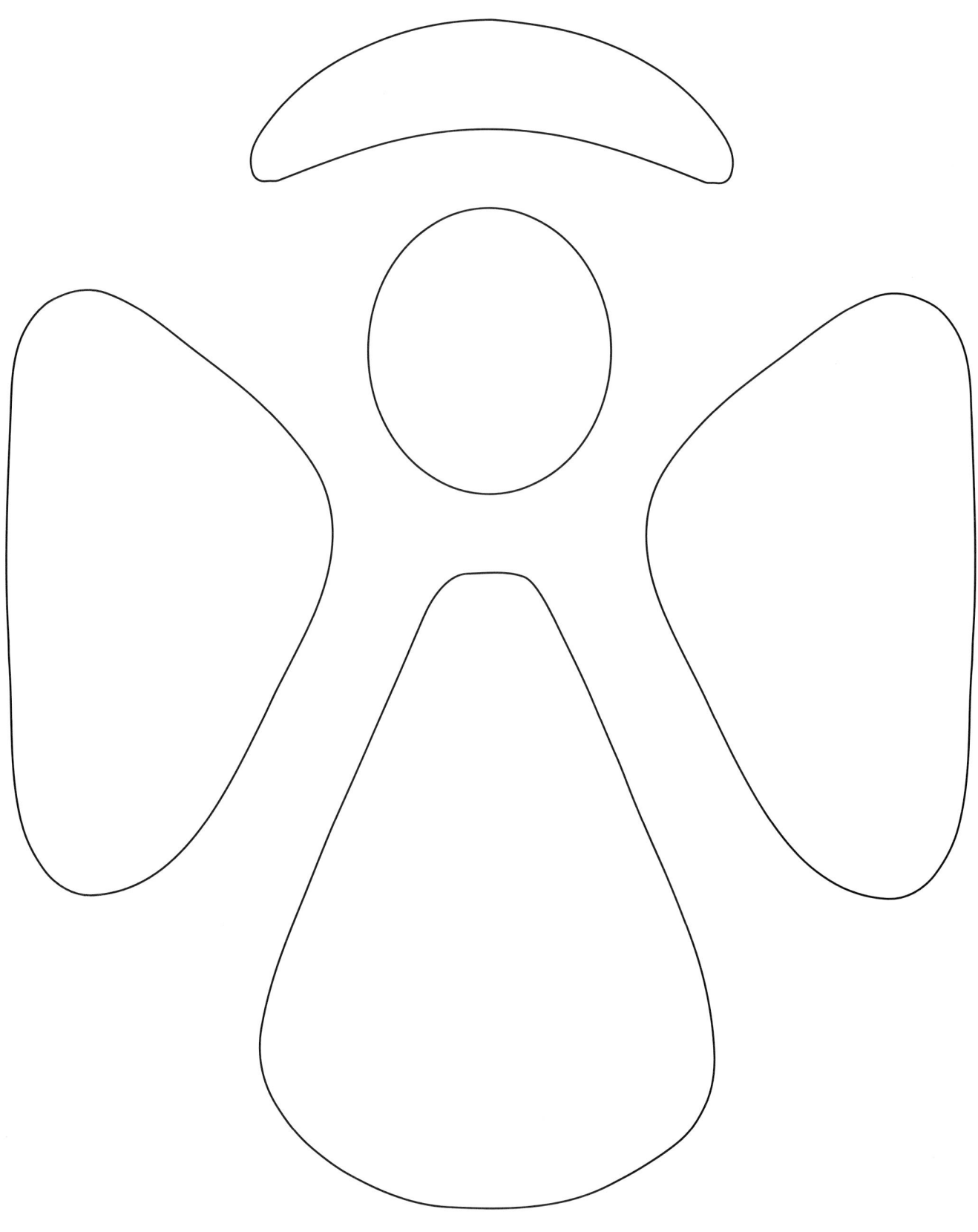

Angel Pattern

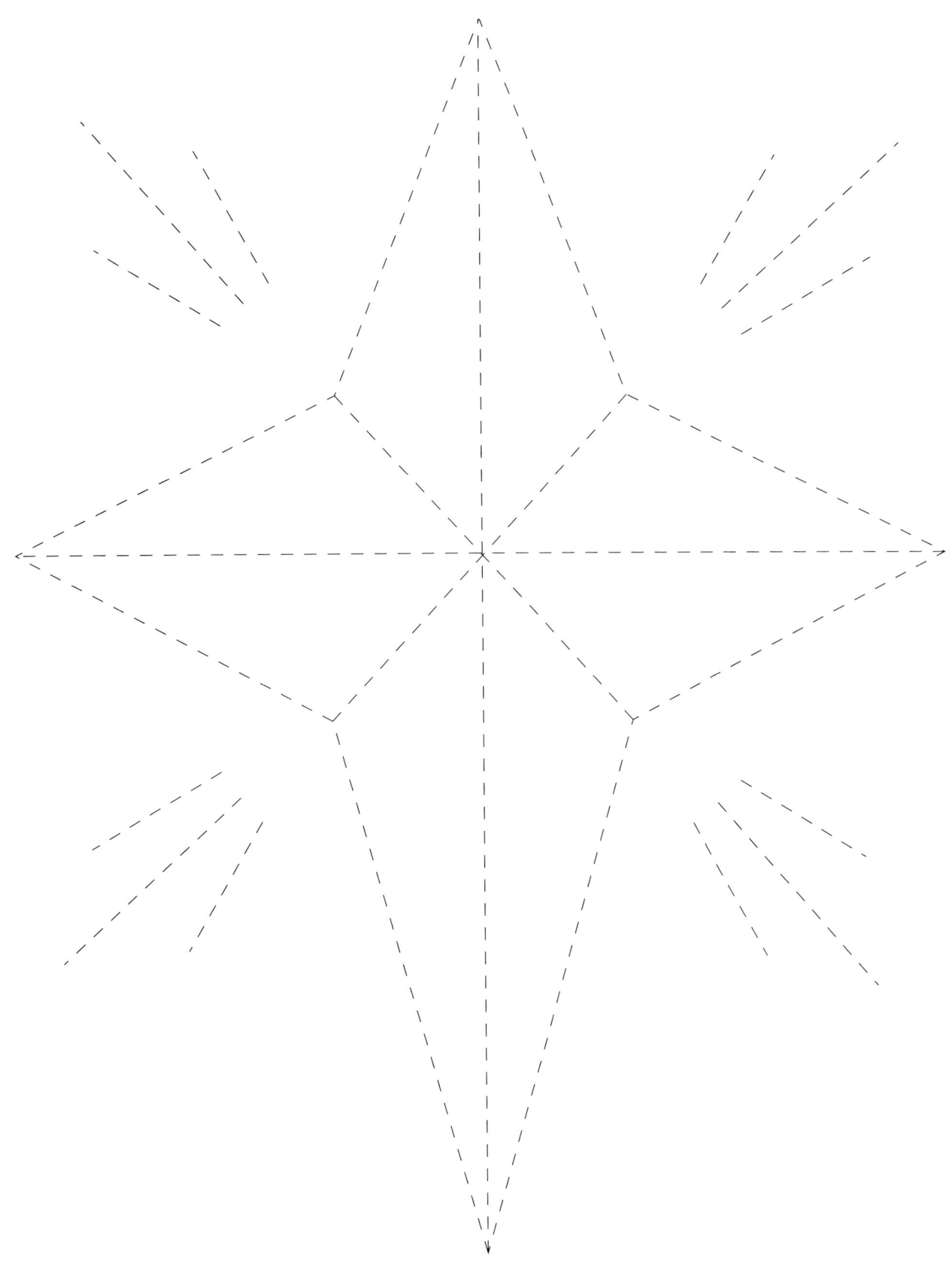

Star Quilting Pattern

*Quilt by Joanne Ramey Cage
Birmingham, Alabama*

Pine Tree Wall Hanging

This wall hanging combines pine green and berry red fabrics in a traditional patchwork tribute to evergreens. Topped off with star-spangled sashing and holly-leaf quilting, it's a holiday decoration that stays fresh throughout the season.

Finished Quilt Size
52" x 52"

Number of Blocks and Finished Size
4 blocks 20" x 20"

Fabric Requirements
Red print   ½ yard
Green print 1½ yards*
White   2½ yards
Backing   3⅛ yards

*Includes fabric for binding.

Number to Cut**

Template A	152 green print
	80 red print
	40 white
Template B	8 red print
	4 white
Template C	4 white
Template C rev.	4 white
Template D	4 green print
Template E	4 white
Template F	4 white
Template G	4 green print
	4 red print
8⅞" square (H)	6 white
	2 green print

**See Step 1 to cut borders and sashing before cutting other pieces.

Quilt Top Assembly

1. From white, cut 2 (4½" x 54") and 2 (4½" x 45") lengthwise strips for border, and 4 (4½" x 20½") lengthwise strips for sashing. Set aside.

2. For H, cut each 8⅞" square in half diagonally to get 12 white triangles and 4 green triangles.

3. Join 1 green A to each C and C rev. as shown in **Diagram 1**. Join A/C units to both sides of each D rectangle. Stitch 1 green H to top of each unit as shown. Press all seam allowances toward green.

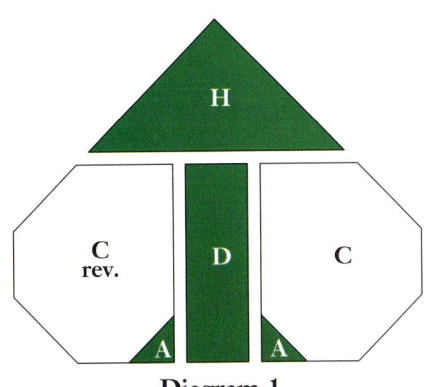

Diagram 1

Diagram 2

Diagram 3

4. Referring to **Diagram 2**, join 3 green As to 3 white As to make 3 green/white triangle-squares. Join squares in a row as shown, adding green A to end of row. For second and third rows of unit, make 9 red/green triangle-squares in same manner and join as shown, adding 1 green A to end of each row. Join 3 rows to make left section of tree. Join to tree trunk unit.

5. Assemble right section of tree in 3 rows as shown in **Diagram 3**, joining 7 green/white triangle-squares, 11 red/green triangle-squares, 3 green As, 2 red Bs, and 1 white B. Join assembled unit to tree trunk unit.

6. Referring to **Diagram 4**, join 3 H triangles to sides and bottom of tree to complete each block.

Diagram 4

Diagram 5

Diagram 6

7. Repeat steps 4–6 to complete a total of 4 pine tree blocks.

8. For center star block, join red and green Gs in pairs as shown in **Diagram 5**. Join pairs to make star halves; then join halves to complete star. Set in Es and Fs as shown in **Diagram 6**. (See page 6, Step 8, for tips on sewing set-in seams.)

9. Referring to **Setting Diagram**, join blocks in 2 rows with a sashing strip between each pair of blocks. Join remaining sashing strips to opposite sides of star block. Press seam allowances toward sashing. Join rows with sashing row between block rows.

10. Join shorter border strips to quilt sides; then join long border strips to top and bottom edges.

Quilting

The quilt shown has a holly leaf design quilted in the borders. Make a stencil from holly pattern on page 25 and mark design on quilt. Draw a wavy line through each sashing strip. Outline-quilt patchwork and marked designs. Add other quilting as desired.

Finishing

Referring to instructions on page 11, make 6 yards of 2"-wide bias or straight-grain binding from green print. Apply binding to quilt edges.

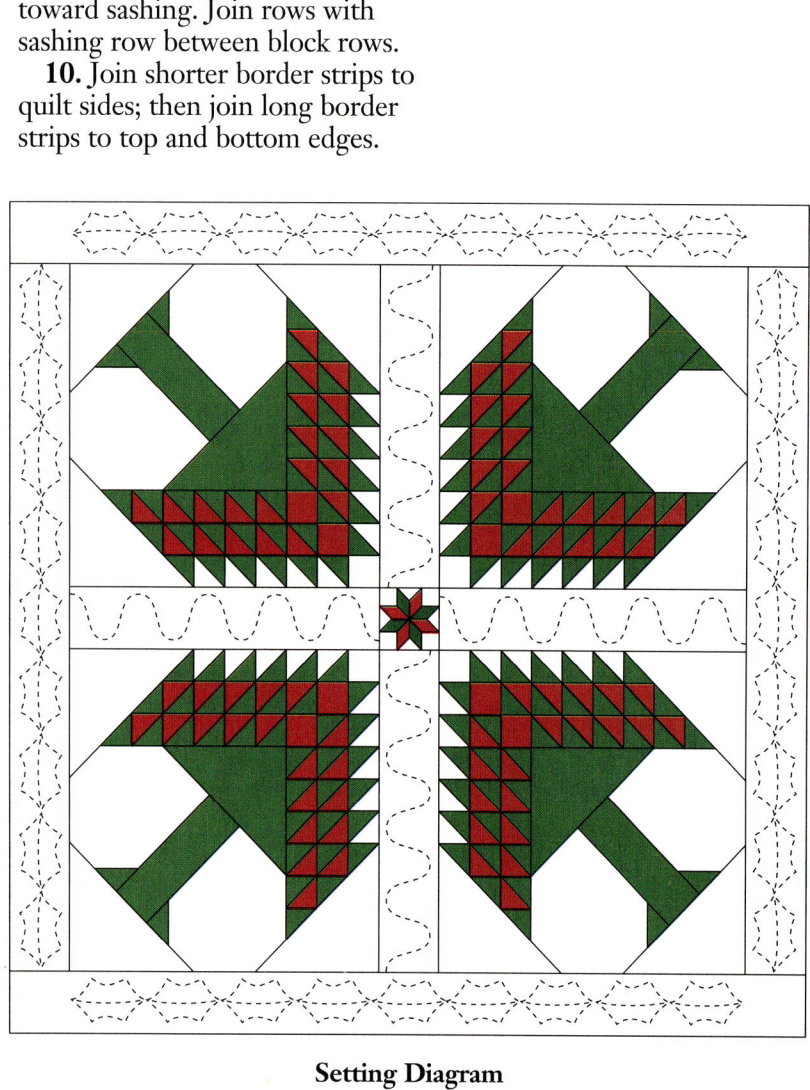

Setting Diagram

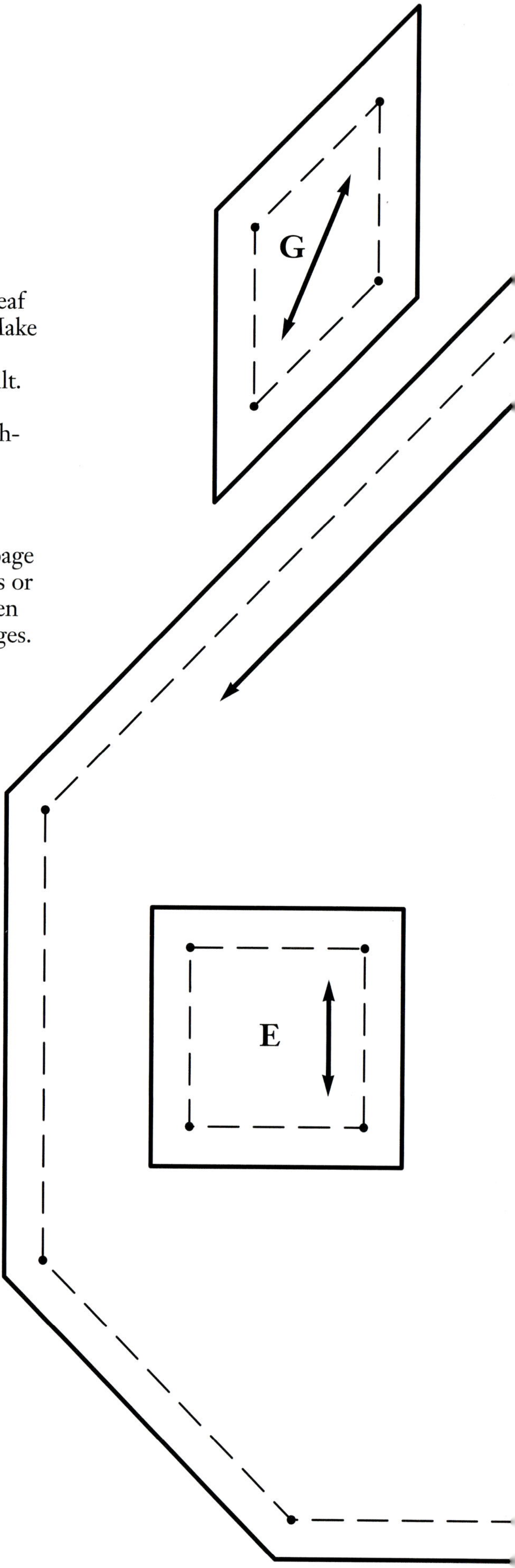

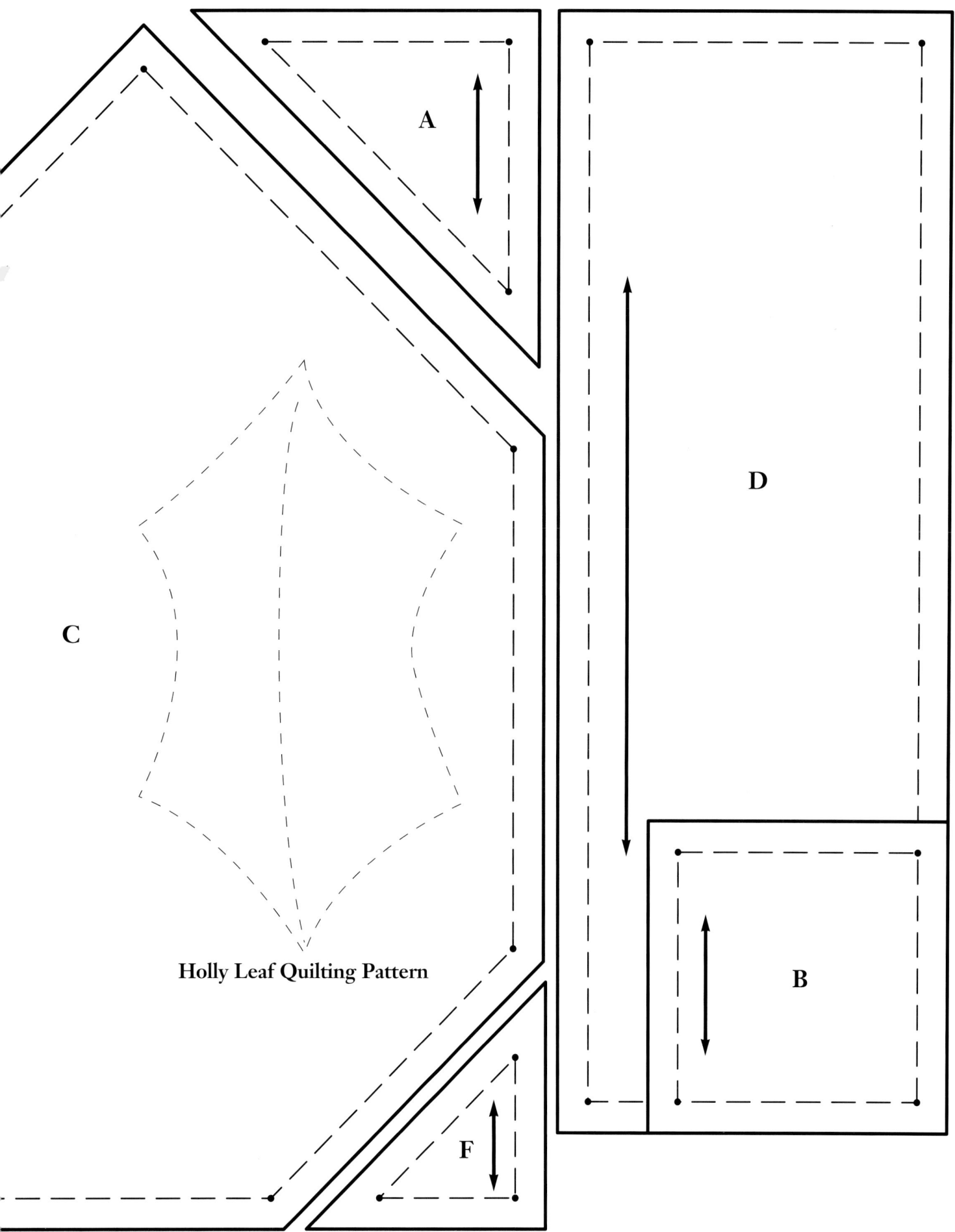
Holly Leaf Quilting Pattern

Stepping Stones

The patchwork pathways of this classic quilt create the illusion of ripe berries sprinkled on a field of gleaming snow. Our quilt is an elegant combination of red and white, but you can choose to be more daring with the fabrics—use a mix of red scraps instead of just one print, or reverse the placement of red and white for a dramatic look. With optional timesaving techniques and rotary cutting, you can get the piecing done between Christmas and New Year's Eve.

*Quilt by Annie C. Phillips
Hayden, Alabama*

Finished Quilt Size
82" x 100"

Number of Blocks and Finished Size
12 blocks   16" x 16"

Fabric Requirements
Red print   3¾ yards
Muslin   7¼ yards*
Backing   6 yards

*Includes fabric for binding.

Number to Cut**
Template A   96 muslin†
                  268 red print†
Template B   96 muslin†
Template C   192 muslin
Template D   48 red print
Template D rev.   48 red print
Template E   12 red print
Template F   200 muslin
Template G   16 muslin

**See Step 1 to cut borders and sashing before cutting other pieces.

† See Alternate Quick Piecing instructions before cutting.

Quilt Top Assembly

1. From red print, cut 2 (2½" x 98") and 2 (2½" x 84") lengthwise strips for outer border. From muslin, cut 2 (4½" x 98") and 2 (4½" x 72") lengthwise strips for middle border, and 2 (4½" x 85") and 2 (4½" x 58") lengthwise strips for inner border. Also from muslin, cut 16 (2½" x 44") crossgrain strips; from these, cut 31 (2½" x 16½") sashing strips. Set aside.

2. Join 8 red As to 8 muslin As. Press seam allowances toward red.

3. Referring to **Block Assembly Diagram,** join A/A units in pairs to make 4 four-patch units. Add 1 B to 1 side of each four-patch as shown.

4. Join 1 red A to each of 4 Bs. Press seam allowances toward A. Join A/B units to each four-patch as shown.

5. Join Cs to ends of 4 Ds and 4 Ds rev. Press seam allowances toward Ds. Join C/D/C units in 4 pairs as shown.

6. Referring to diagram, lay out assembled units in 3 horizontal rows. Join units in each row; then join rows to complete 1 block.

Alternate Quick Piecing

If you're short of time or if marking and cutting just isn't your thing, take a shortcut to reduce marking, cutting, and sewing time. In this block, pieces for corner units can be rotary-cut and quick-pieced. For this method, templates are not used to cut A and B. (But you will need to cut 124 As separately for sashing and border.)

1. Cut 9 (2½" x 43") strips of red print and 6 matching strips of muslin. Also cut 6 (4½"-wide) muslin strips.

2. Join red strips to 2½"-wide muslin strips and 3 (4½"-wide) muslin strips to make 9 strip sets. Press seam allowances toward red.

3. Referring to **Rotary Cutting Diagram,** cut 16 (2½"-wide) segments from each strip set to get 96 A/A units and 48 A/B units.

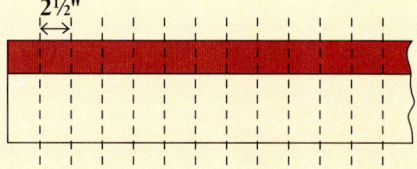

Rotary Cutting Diagram

4. From remaining muslin strips, cut 48 (2½"-wide) segments for Bs.

5. Follow steps 3–6 to complete blocks.

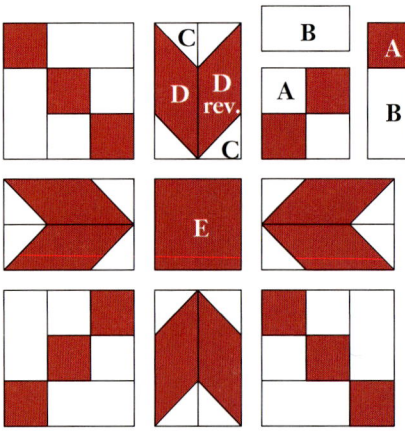

Block Assembly Diagram

7. Repeat steps 2–6 to make a total of 12 blocks.

8. Referring to **Setting Diagram,** lay out blocks in 4 horizontal rows of 3 blocks with sashing strips between blocks. Join blocks and sashing in each row. Add sashing strips to row ends. Press seam allowances toward sashing.

9. For each horizontal sashing row, join 4 red As and 3 sashing strips as shown. Make 5 sashing rows. Press seam allowances toward sashing.

10. Join block rows and sashing rows as shown.

11. Join 58" muslin borders to top and bottom edges of quilt. Trim borders even with quilt sides; then press seam allowances toward borders.

12. Measure length of quilt through the middle. Trim 85" muslin borders to this length, but do not join yet.

13. Referring to **Border Piecing Diagram,** join red As to Fs and Gs to make units for middle borders. Using a scant ¼" seam, make 28 G/A/F units for each side border. Join units to make border strip. Compare length of pieced borders with trimmed muslin borders; then adjust piecing as necessary to make borders match. Join pieced borders to muslin borders as shown; then join border unit to quilt sides.

Border Piecing Diagram

Setting Diagram

14. Join 24 G/A/F units each for top and bottom border in same manner as for side borders. Adjust seams as necessary to fit borders to width of quilt. Join pieced borders to top and bottom edges of quilt.

15. Join 72" border strips to top and bottom edges.

16. Matching long edges, join 98"-long red and muslin borders. Add these units to quilt sides as shown. Join remaining red borders to top and bottom edges.

Quilting

Use a purchased stencil to mark a 3"-wide cable design in muslin borders. Outline-quilt patchwork and sashing; then quilt marked borders.

Finishing

Referring to instructions on page 11, make 10¼ yards of 2½"-wide bias or straight-grain binding from remaining muslin. Apply binding to quilt edges.

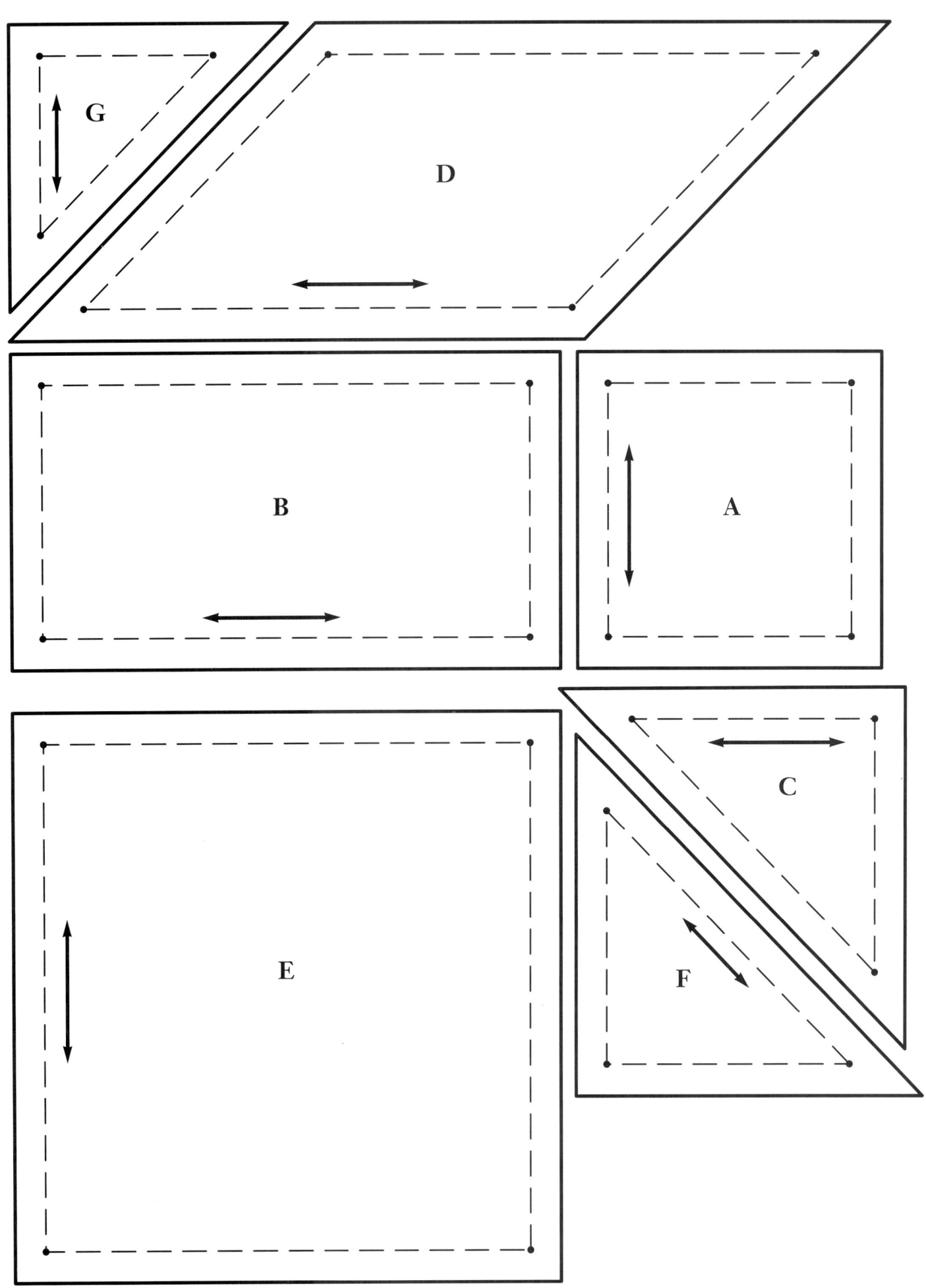

Quilt by Dorothy Repass Umberger
Ceres, Virginia

Christmas Beauty

Classic geometry and holiday fabrics make this a quilt for all seasons. A variation of a traditional Irish Chain, the checkerboard units are strip-pieced, while patterns are given for the center triangles and the Flying Geese border.

Finished Quilt Size
77¾" x 92¾"

Number of Blocks and Finished Size
20 blocks   16" x 16"

Fabric Requirements
Red paisley   1½ yards
Green paisley   1½ yards
Muslin   4 yards
Red   1½ yards
Green   1¾ yards*
Backing   5½ yards

*Includes fabric for binding.

Number to Cut
Template A   80 red paisley
                80 green paisley
                160 muslin
Template B   67 red paisley
                67 green paisley
Template C   236 muslin

Quilt Top Assembly

1. For checkerboard units, cut 10 (2½"-wide) crossgrain strips from green, 10 strips from red, and 20 strips from muslin. Join 1 muslin strip to each colored strip to make 20 strip sets. Press seam allowances toward darker fabric.

2. Cut each strip set into 16 (2½"-wide) segments, as shown in **Diagram 1,** to get 160 segments of each color combination.

3. Referring to **Diagram 2,** join 2 green segments to make 1 checkerboard unit. In this manner, make 80 green/muslin units and 80 red/muslin units.

4. Join all paisley As to muslin As to get 160 pieced squares. Press seam allowances toward paisleys.

5. Referring to **Block Assembly Diagram,** lay out assembled units in 4 horizontal rows. Join units in each row; then join rows to complete 1 block. Repeat to make a total of 20 blocks.

6. Referring to photograph, lay out blocks in 5 horizontal rows of 4 blocks. Join blocks in each row.

7. From red, cut 4 (1¾"-wide) and 4 (2¼"-wide) crossgrain strips. Join 2 narrow strips end-to-end. Matching centers, sew pieced strip to top edge of quilt. Repeat for bottom border. Join pairs of wider strips for side borders. Sew these to quilt in same manner and miter corners.

8. Referring to **Diagram 3,** join Cs to sides of each B to make 1 Flying Geese unit. Make 118 units.

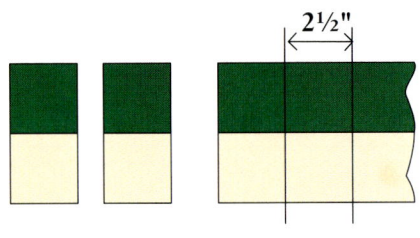

Diagram 1

Diagram 2

Block Assembly Diagram

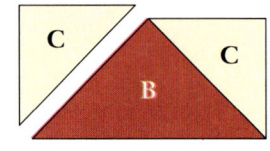

Diagram 3

9. Alternating colors, join 17 red units and 16 green units to make a pieced border for left side of quilt. Row begins and ends with a red unit. Make right side border in same manner, using 17 green units and 16 red units so that row begins and ends with green. Join pieced borders to quilt sides, easing as necessary to fit.

10. Beginning with a red unit, join 13 red units and 13 green units in same manner for top border. Repeat for bottom border, beginning with a green unit.

11. Join remaining Bs in pairs as shown in **Diagram 4,** always sewing red to green. Join pairs as shown to make 4 corner squares. Referring to photograph, join corner squares to each end of top and bottom borders, positioning squares to maintain alternation of colors. Join pieced borders to top and bottom edges of quilt as shown, easing as necessary to fit.

Diagram 4

Quilting

Outline-quilt patchwork. Add other quilting as desired. Quilt shown has stipple quilting in each muslin triangle that outlines a hand-drawn paisley.

Finishing

Referring to instructions on page 11, make 10 yards of 2½"-wide bias or straight-grain binding from remaining green. Apply binding to quilt edges.

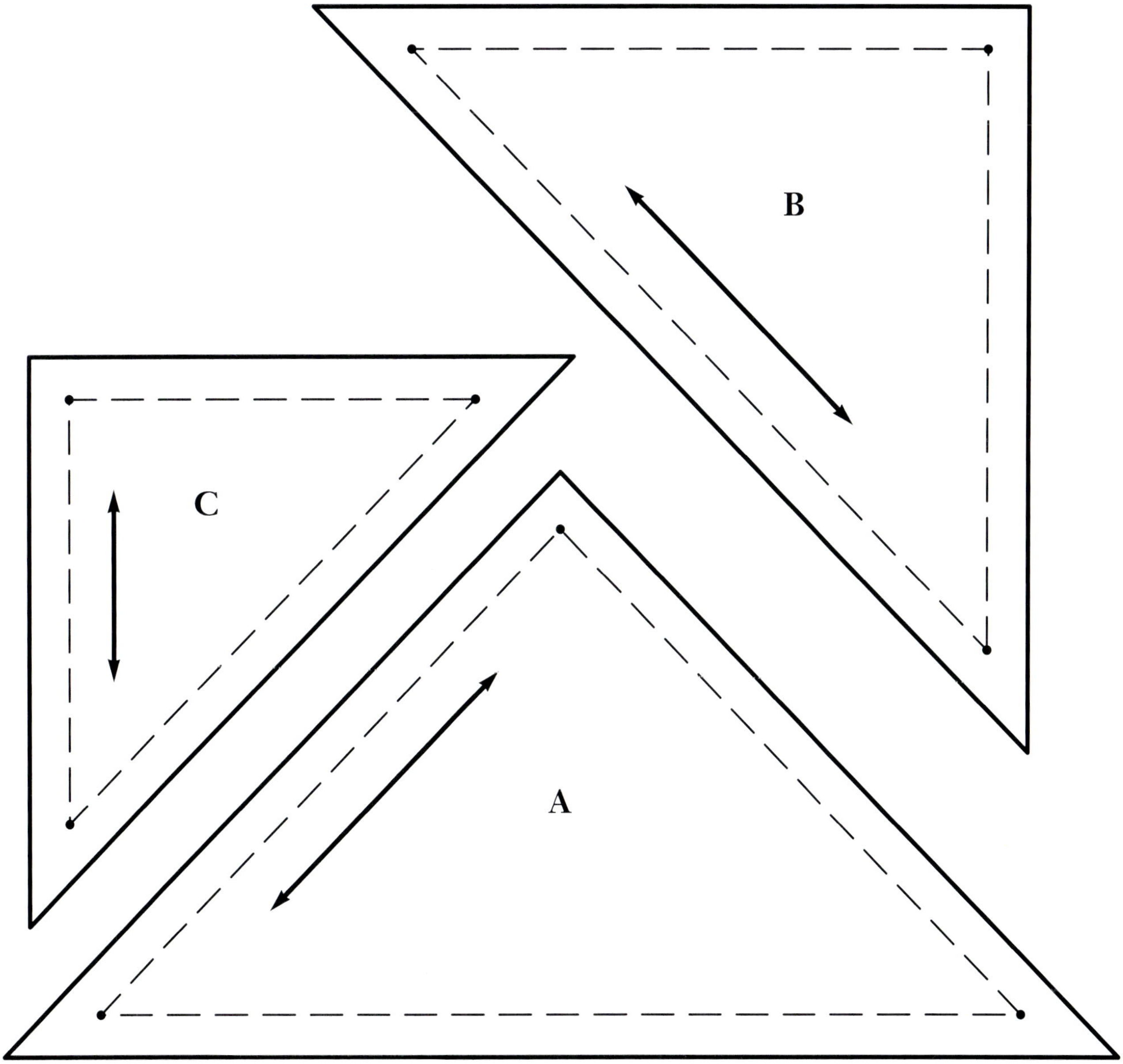

*Quilt by Jane Golden Strickland
Linden, Alabama*

Night Before Christmas

Use preprinted fabrics to incorporate the sights and scenes of Christmas into an easy-to-make quilt of patchwork stars. Every year, fabric stores offer exciting new selections of preprinted panels like these that illustrate Clement Moore's classic poem. Let one of them inspire your holiday quilt.

Finished Quilt Size
40" x 52"

Number of Blocks and Finished Size
6 star blocks   12" x 12"

Fabric Requirements
Preprinted panels
Green print   ½ yard
Muslin   ½ yard
Red print   ¾ yard
Backing   1½ yards

Number to Cut*
Template A   72 muslin
                   36 green print
                   36 red print
3½" squares (B)   12 green print
                   12 red print
2½" squares   8 green print
12½" squares   6 preprinted panels

*See Step 1 to cut borders before cutting other pieces.

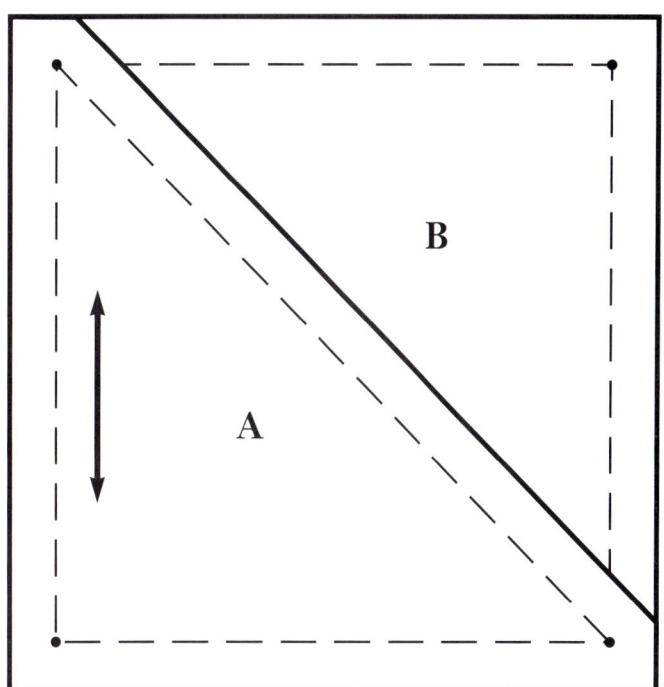

Quilt Top Assembly

1. From red print, cut 4 (2½" x 24") and 4 (2½" x 18") crossgrain strips for border. Set aside.

2. Referring to **Block 1 Assembly Diagram**, join muslin As to 4 green print As and 8 red print As to make 12 triangle-squares. Press seam allowances toward prints.

3. Arrange triangle-squares and 4 green print Bs in 4 horizontal rows as shown. Join squares in each row; then join rows to complete block. Repeat to make a total of 3 of Block 1.

4. Referring to **Block 2 Assembly Diagram**, make 3 of Block 2 in same manner.

5. Referring to photograph and **Setting Diagram**, arrange blocks and preprinted blocks in 4 horizontal rows of 3 blocks. Join blocks in each row; then join rows.

6. Referring to **Setting Diagram**, join each pair of 24" borders with a 2½" green print square between them. Join these borders to sides of quilt. Press seam allowances toward borders.

7. Join 18" border strips with 3 green print squares as shown for top and bottom borders. Sew borders to quilt.

Quilting

1. Layer backing (right side down), quilt top (right side up), and batting, in that order. Baste.

2. With batting against feed dogs, machine-stitch around edges, leaving a 12" opening in 1 side. Turn through opening. Slipstitch opening closed.

3. Outline-quilt patchwork. Add other quilting as desired.

Block 1 Assembly Diagram

Block 2 Assembly Diagram

Setting Diagram

Quilt by Carol Wight Jones
North Attleboro, Massachusetts

Christmas Cactus

Nature dresses up for the holidays with plants that flower in an otherwise drab season. An old favorite is the Christmas cactus, which often produces bright flowers just in time to greet St. Nick. To keep your spirit in bloom, use freezer paper techniques to appliqué this pattern.

Finished Quilt Size
38" x 38"

Number of Blocks and Finished Size
4 blocks   14" x 14"

Fabric Requirements
Green print   1⅛ yards
Muslin   1 yard
Red   1 yard
Green for binding   ⅝ yard
Backing   1¼ yards

Other Materials
Freezer paper

Number to Cut*
Template A   16 red
Template A rev.   16 red
Template B   80 red
15" squares   4 muslin
12½" squares   4 green print
     4 freezer paper

*See Step 1 to cut borders and sashing before cutting other pieces.

Quilt Top Assembly

1. From red, cut 6 (2½"-wide) crossgrain strips. From these, cut 2 (17"-long) strips and 1 (35"-long) strip for sashing and 4 (39"-long) strips for border. Set aside.

2. With dull side out, fold 1 freezer paper square in fourths. Referring to **Placement Diagram**, lay cactus template on paper as shown and trace. Cut out paper pattern on drawn line, cutting through all layers. Be careful not to cut center where 4 stems meet.

3. With coated side down, center paper pattern on wrong side of 1 green print square. Using a dry iron, press pattern onto fabric.

4. Center green print square, with paper pattern on back, on right side of 1 muslin square. Pin at corners. Starting at 1 corner of cactus, remove pin and carefully cut green print around paper shape, leaving ¼" seam allowances. Cut about a 3" section; then appliqué that section, using tip of needle to turn seam allowance over paper edge. Clip seam allowances as necessary. Continue trimming and appliquéing, 1 section at a time, until appliqué is complete.

5. Referring to photograph, appliqué 4 As and 4 As rev. to square, positioning 1 on each side of wide cactus blades. Appliqué 20 Bs in place as shown. When complete, carefully slit muslin behind appliqué and remove freezer paper. (Use a needle or tweezers to gently pull out paper in sections.) Square up and trim appliquéd blocks to 14½" x 14½".

6. Repeat steps 2–5 to make a total of 4 appliquéd blocks.

7. From remaining green print, cut 8 (1½" x 14½") strips and 8 (1½" x 16½") strips for sashing. Join 1 shorter strip to opposite sides of each block. Press seam allowances toward sashing. Join longer strips to remaining sides.

8. Join blocks in 2 rows of 2 blocks with 1 (17") red sashing strip between each pair. Join rows with 35" red sashing strip between rows.

9. Join borders to quilt, mitering corners.

Quilting
Quilt a vein down the center of each large cactus leaf. Echo-quilt cactus design, beginning ¼" from seam line and extending out to block seam lines. Quilting lines are ¼" apart. Quilt borders as desired.

Finishing
Referring to instructions on page 11, make 4½ yards of 2"-wide bias or straight-grain binding from green. Apply binding to quilt edges.

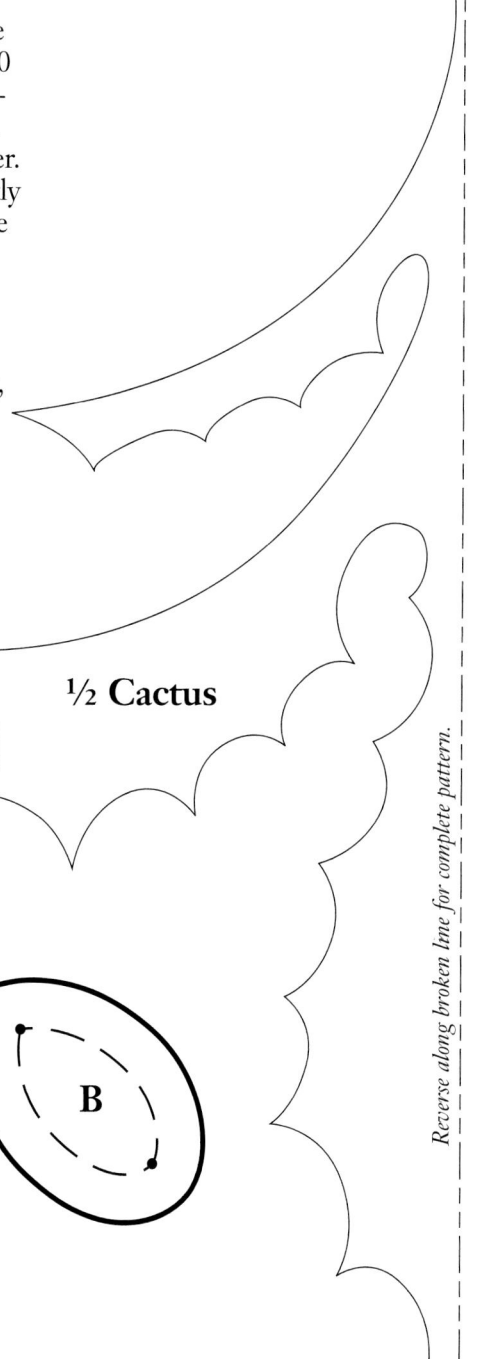

½ Cactus

Reverse along broken line for complete pattern.

Placement Diagram

Dull Side of Freezer Paper

A

B

*Quilt by Carol Butzke
Slinger, Wisconsin*

Visions of Santa

Inspired by Victorian cards and ornaments depicting Father Christmas, the pattern for this friendship quilt was adapted from a soft sculpture doll. The maker of each appliquéd block personalized her Santa, giving him different things to wear or to carry.

Finished Quilt Size
96" x 96"

Number of Blocks and Finished Size
25 blocks   12" x 12"

Fabric Requirements
Dark green   3¾ yards*
Green   2 yards
Red   2½ yards
Muslin   3¼ yards
Black   ¼ yard
Peach   ⅛ yard
"Fur"**   scraps
Assorted solids scraps
Assorted prints scraps
Backing   8¾ yards

*Includes fabric for binding.

**Fur may be fake fur, fleece, or other fabric suitable for hat/coat trim and beard.

Other Materials
Black embroidery floss

Pieces to Cut†
Template A   25 black
Template B   25 black
Template C††   16 assorted solids
Template D††   25 fur
Template E††   25 fur
Template F   25 assorted solids
Template G††   25 fur
Template H   8 assorted prints
Template I   8 assorted prints
Template J   8 assorted prints
Template K††   16 assorted solids
Template L   25 assorted solids
Template M††   25 fur
Template N††   25 assorted solids
Template O   25 peach
Template P††   25 fur
Template Q   25 fur
Template R   9 assorted prints
Template S   9 assorted prints
Template T   9 assorted prints
Template U††   9 assorted solids
Template V   8 assorted prints
Template W   64 green
Template X   240 red
Template Y   24 red
12½" squares   25 muslin

†See Step 1 to cut borders and sashing before cutting other pieces.

††For each block, cut coat, hat, and sleeve from same fabric. For each block, cut all fur except beard from same fabric.

Quilt Top Assembly

1. From red, cut 4 (1¼" x 90") lengthwise strips for inner border and 128 (1¼" x 13¼") strips for block borders.

2. To make appliqué placement guidelines, fold 1 muslin background square in half diagonally and finger-press. Unfold square; fold in half along opposite diagonal and finger-press. Repeat to mark all background squares.

3. Following **Bag Santa Placement Diagram,** appliqué pieces to 1 background square in order: 1 A, 1 B, 1 C, 1 D, 1 E, 1 F, 1 G, 1 H, 1 I, 1 J, 1 K, 1 L, 1 M, 1 N, 1 O, 1 P, and 1 Q. Using 2 strands of black embroidery floss, outline-stitch eyebrows, nose, mustache, and ribbons on gifts H and I. (See stitch diagrams on page 41.) Satin-stitch eyes. Repeat to make a total of 8 Bag Santa blocks.

4. Following **Wreath Santa Placement Diagram,** appliqué pieces to 1 background square in order: 1 A, 1 B, 1 C, 1 D, 1 E, 1 F, 1 G, 1 N, 1 O, 1 P, 1 Q, 1 K, 1 V, 1 L, and 1 M. Using 2 strands of black embroidery floss, outline-stitch eyebrows, nose, and mustache. Satin-stitch eyes. Repeat to make a total of 8 Wreath Santa blocks.

5. Following **Basket Santa Placement Diagram,** appliqué pieces to 1 background square in order: 1 A, 1 B, 1 U, 1 D, 1 E, 1 F, 1 G, 1 N, 1 O, 1 P, 1 Q, 1 R, 1 S, 1 T, 1 L, and 1 M. Using 2 strands of black embroidery floss, outline-stitch eyebrows, nose, mustache, ribbons on gifts R and S, and band on basket T. Satin-stitch eyes. Repeat to make a total of 9 Basket Santa blocks.

Bag Santa Appliqué Placement Diagram—Make 8.

Wreath Santa Appliqué Placement Diagram—Make 8.

Basket Santa Appliqué Placement Diagram—Make 9.

Setting Diagram

Sashing Strip Assembly Diagram

6. Join 2 (13¼") red strips to opposite sides of each block. Trim strips and press seam allowances toward red. Join 2 more strips to remaining sides of each block in same manner.

7. For sashing, join red Xs to each end of 36 green Ws as shown in **Sashing Strip Assembly Diagram.** Then join Xs to 1 end only for another 24 Ws. Press seam allowances toward red.

8. From dark green, cut 4 (4½" x 99") lengthwise strips for outer border and set aside. From remainder, cut 3 (16¾") squares and 2 (9") squares. Cut larger squares into quarters diagonally to get 12 side triangles. Cut smaller squares in half diagonally to get 4 corner triangles.

9. Referring to **Setting Diagram,** join block border strips to short legs of each side triangle, mitering corners as shown.

10. Referring to **Setting Diagram,** lay out blocks, side triangles, corner triangles, remaining block border strips, sashing, and red Ys in diagonal rows. Join remaining Xs to sashing as needed.

11. Join units in each row as shown; then join rows.

12. Join red border strips to quilt, mitering corners. Then join dark green border strips to quilt in same manner.

Quilting

Outline-quilt appliquéd figures. Quilt a 1½" crosshatch pattern on remainder of each block and on each side triangle and corner triangle. Quilt block border strips and sashing strips in-the-ditch. Quilt outer border as desired.

Finishing

Referring to instructions on page 11, make 11 yards of 2½"-wide bias or straight-grain binding from remaining dark green. Apply binding to quilt edges.

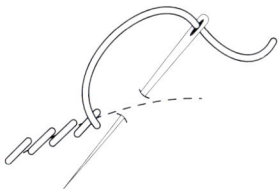
Outline Stitch

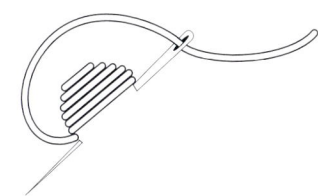
Satin Stitch

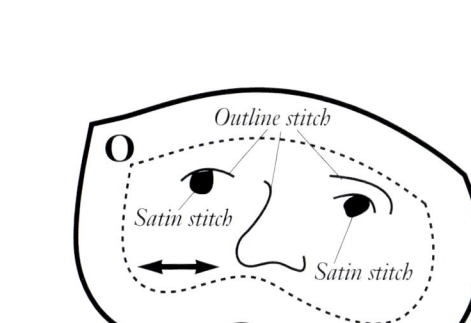

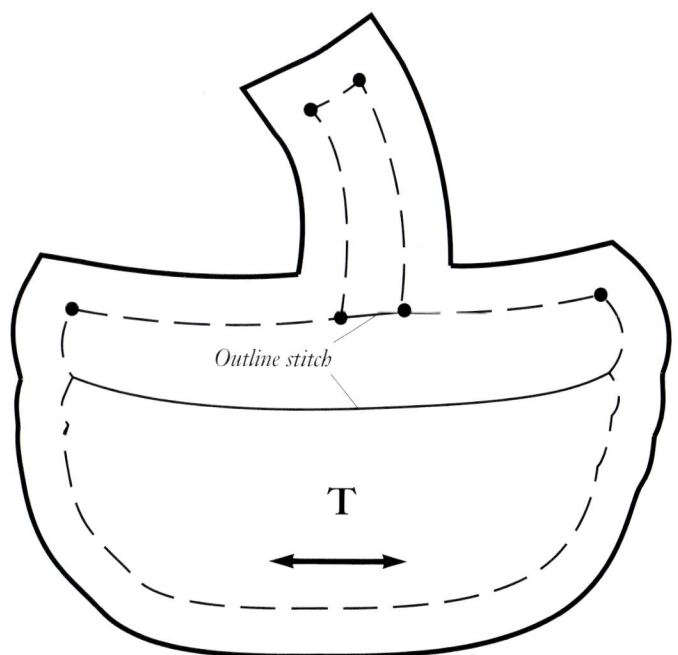

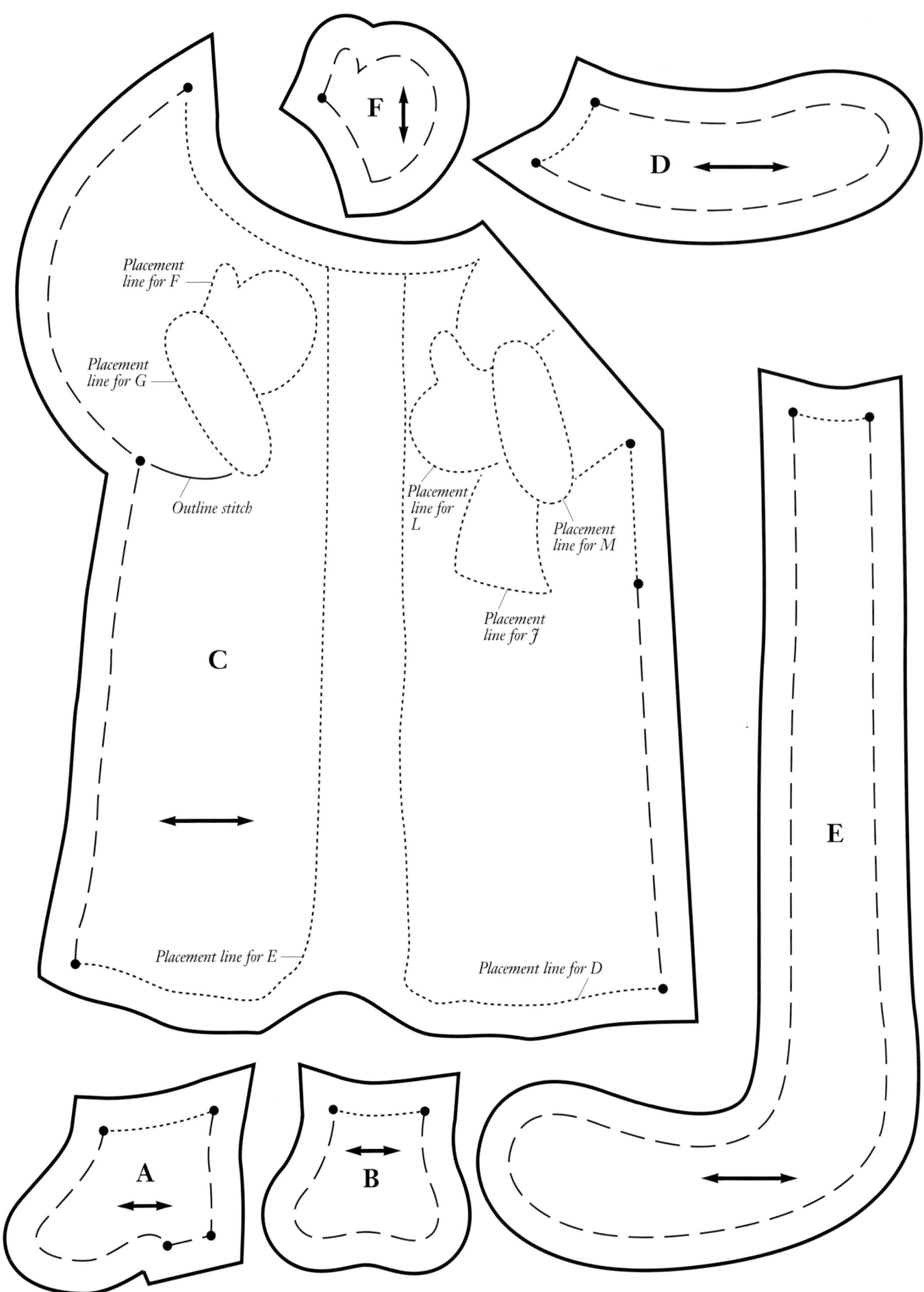

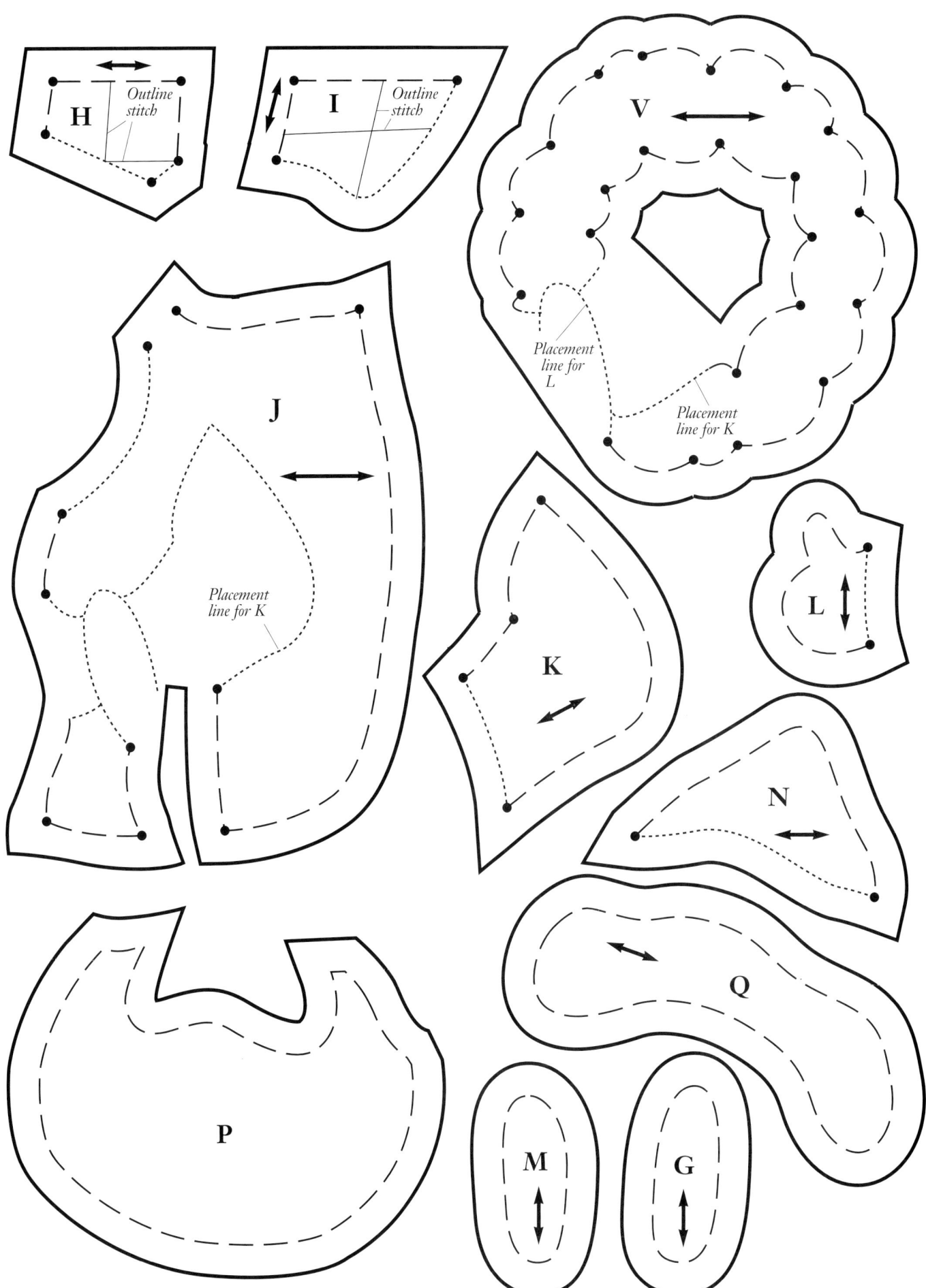

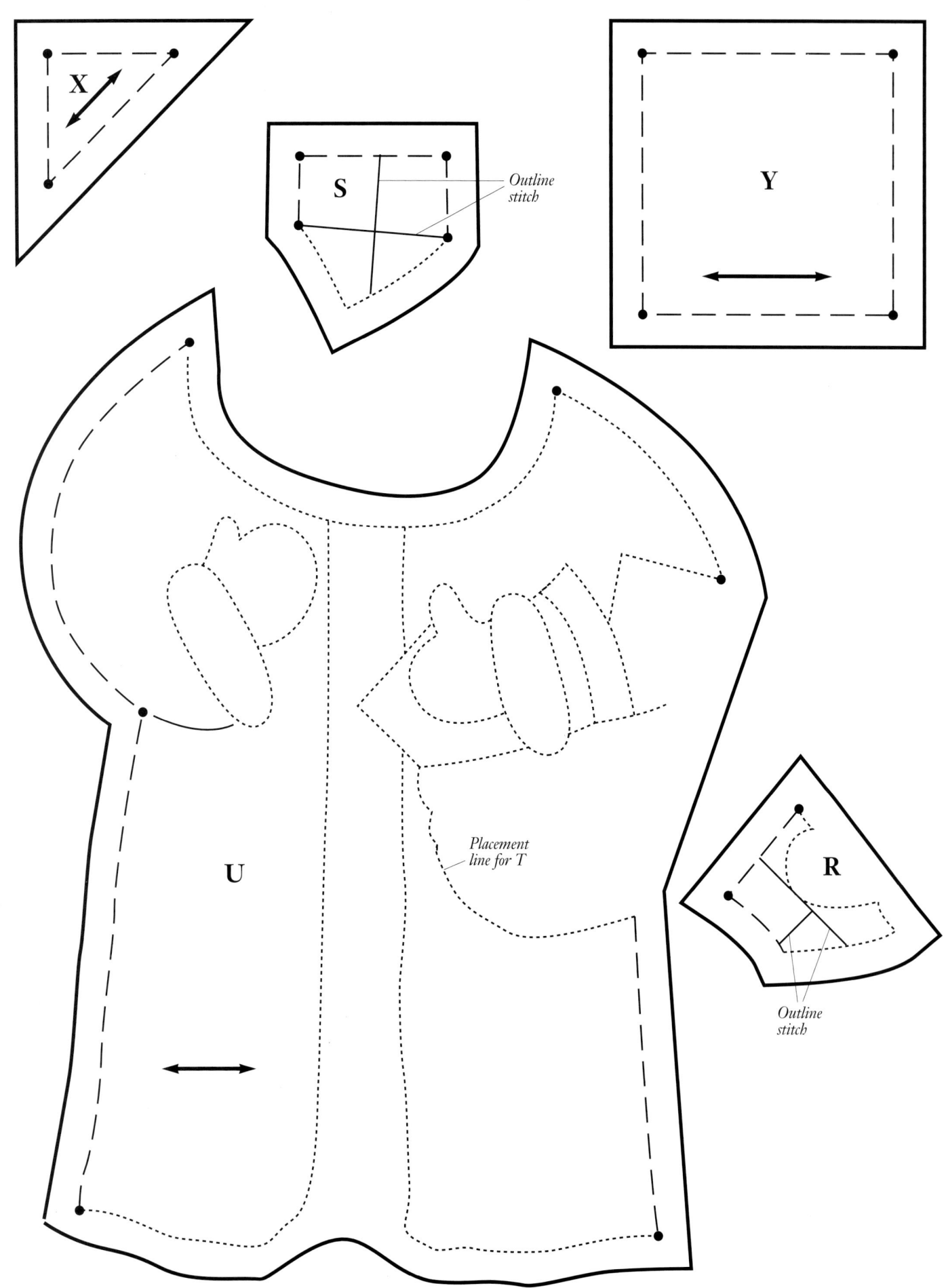

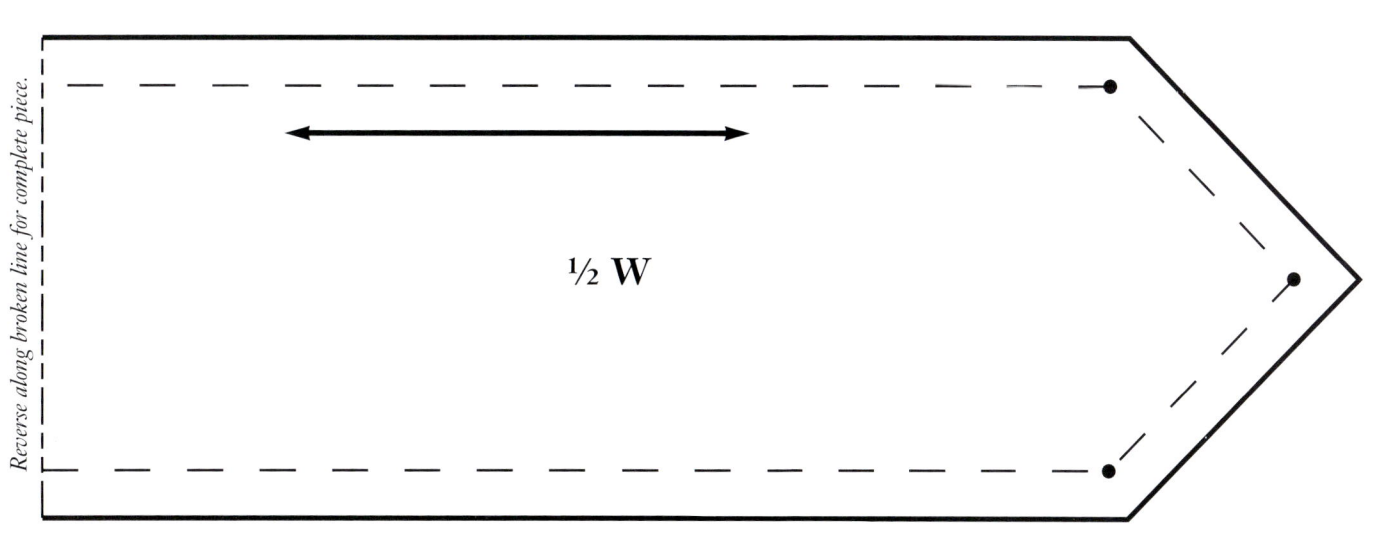

½ W

Reverse along broken line for complete piece.

*Quilt by Shelly Burge
Lincoln, Nebraska*

Christmas Lily

These blooming lilies, framed with a ribbon-like border, are a lovely combination of patchwork and appliqué. Scraps and a clever strip-piecing technique make quick work of the multifaceted diamonds.

Finished Quilt Size
38½" x 38½"

Number of Blocks and Finished Size
1 block   17" x 17"

Fabric Requirements
White   1½ yards
Dark green   1 yard*
Red prints   scraps
Green prints   scraps
Backing   1¼ yards

*Includes fabric for binding.

Number to Cut
Template A**   48 red print
                        8 green print
Template B   40 white
Template C   4 white
Template D   2 white
Template D rev.   2 white
Template E   8 green print
9" square   1 white
14½" squares   2 white

**See Step 1 for strip-piecing instructions before cutting.

Diagram 1

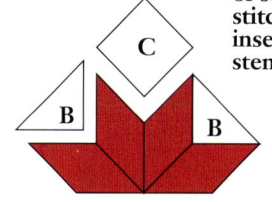
Diagram 2

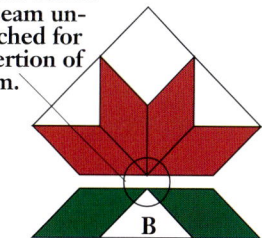
Diagram 3   Diagram 4

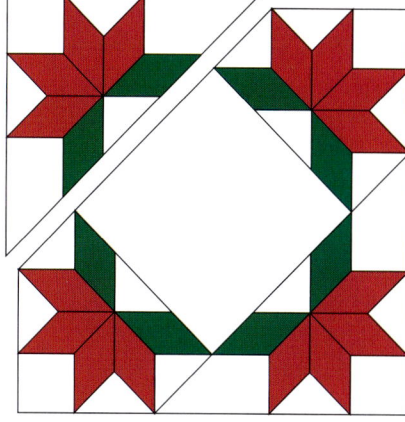
Diagram 5

Diagram 6

Quilt Top Assembly

1. Cut strips from red prints, varying widths from ¾" wide to 2" wide. Join strips to make a patchwork about 7" wide. Referring to **Diagram 1,** lay Template A on patchwork to cut diamonds. You'll need to make 3 (7" x 44") patchwork strips for red diamonds. Make 1 (7" x 22") strip for green diamonds.

2. Join 4 red diamonds as shown in **Diagram 2.** Set 2 Bs and 1 C into openings as shown. (See page 6, Step 8, for tips on sewing set-in seams.) Referring to **Diagram 3,** join 2 green diamonds to opposite sides of 1 B. Press seam allowances toward B. Then join red diamonds to green diamonds as shown, leaving about 1" unstitched at center of seam—this is where stem will be inserted later. Repeat to make a total of 4 lilies.

3. For each of 2 lilies, set in 2 Bs as shown in **Diagram 4.** For each of 2 remaining lilies, set in 1 D and 1 D rev. as shown in **Diagram 5.**

4. Sew first pair of lilies to opposite sides of 9" white square as shown in **Diagram 6.** Join second pair to remaining sides as shown.

5. For bias stems, cut an 8" square of dark green. Cut square in half diagonally to get 2 triangles. Measuring from cut edge of 1 triangle, cut 4 (⅞"-wide) diagonal strips. Be sure each strip is at least 9" long—if not, cut more strips from second triangle as needed. With wrong sides facing, fold each bias strip in half lengthwise and stitch ¼" from raw edges. Trim seam allowances and press to back of strip.

6. Referring to photograph, pin end of each stem in seam opening of 1 lily. Curve stems as shown, hiding end of each strip under neighboring stem, and pin. When satisfied with position of stems, appliqué stems and Es in place on center square. When appliqué is complete, close opening in each lily, enclosing stem ends in seams.

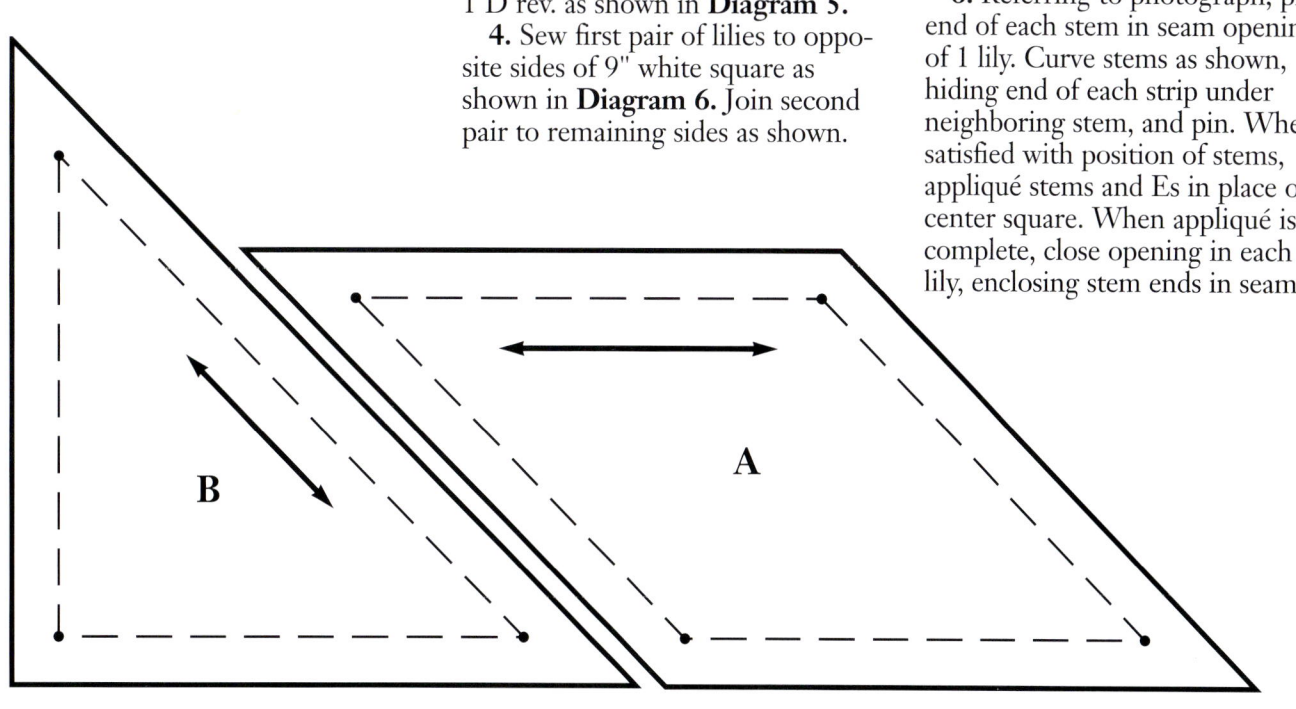

7. From white, cut 2 (2" x 18") strips and sew these to opposite sides of block. Cut 2 (2" x 21") strips and join these to remaining sides.

8. From dark green, cut 4 (2½" x 26") strips. Join these to block in same manner as for white border.

9. Referring to **Setting Diagram,** join 4 red As and 3 Bs to make a pieced border strip. Repeat to make 8 pieced strips. Press seam allowances toward Bs.

10. Cut each 14½" white square in half diagonally to get 4 triangles. Join border strips to triangles as shown, mitering corners.

11. From remaining white, cut 4 (2¾"-wide) strips for outer border. Join borders to quilt in same manner as for inner border.

Quilting

Make or purchase stencils for quilting designs to fit borders and large white triangles. Mark designs on quilt top. Quilt patchwork in-the-ditch; then quilt marked designs. Add background cross-hatching if desired.

Finishing

Referring to instructions on page 11, make 5¾ yards of 2½"-wide bias or straight-grain binding from remaining dark green. Apply binding to quilt edges.

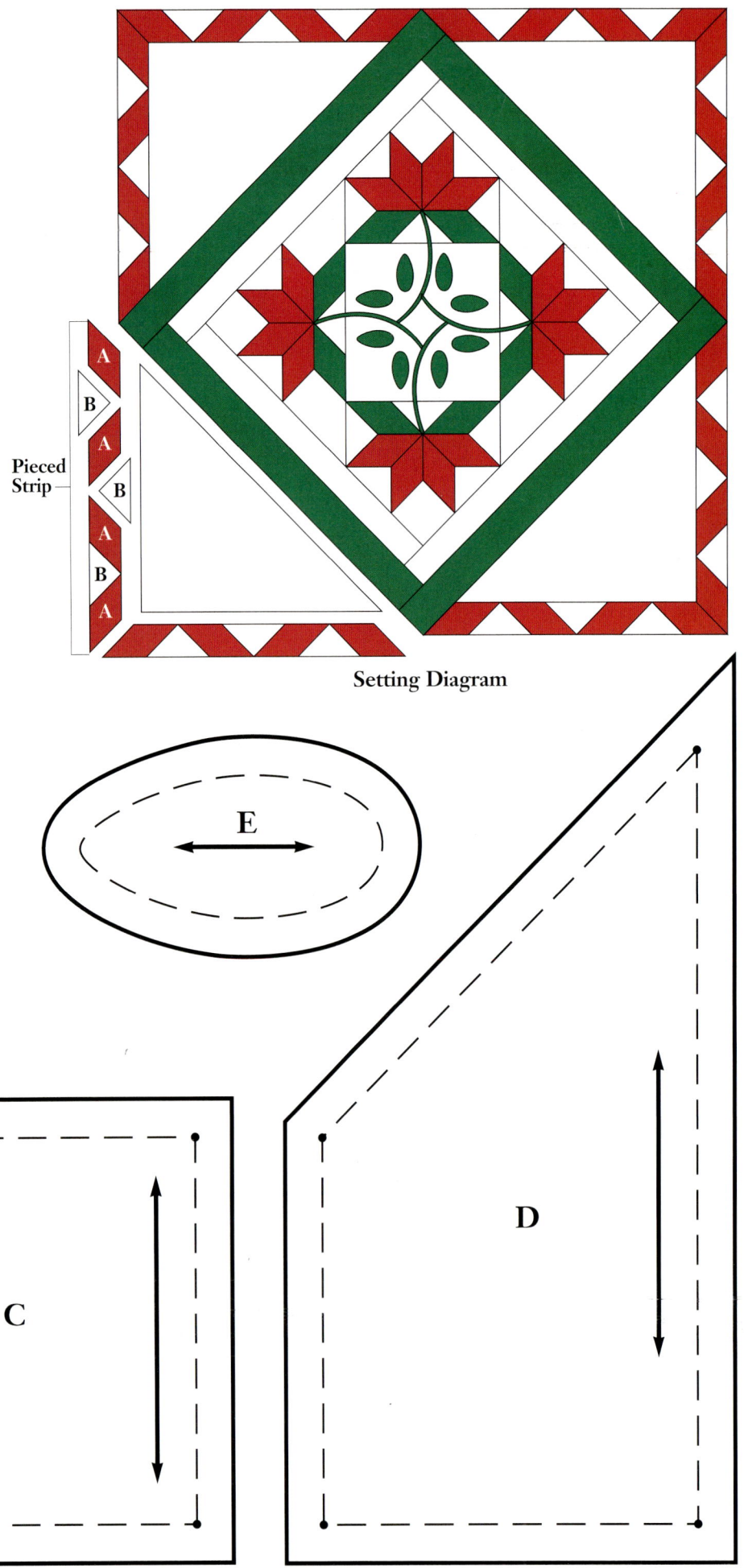

Setting Diagram